The Tuskegee Airmen

BLACK HEROES OF WORLD WAR II

JACQUELINE L. HARRIS

DILLON PRESS
PARSIPPANY, NEW JERSEY

Published by Dillon Press,
A Division of Simon & Schuster
299 Jefferson Road, Parsippany, New Jersey 07054

Designed by Marie Fitzgerald

Manufactured in United States of America
10 9 8 7 6 5 4 3 2 1

Library of Congress Cataloging-in-Publication Data
Harris, Jacqueline L.
The Tuskegee Airmen: Black Heroes of World War II/by Jacqueline L. Harris.
p. cm.
Summary: African Americans battle prejudice at home to become fighter pilots
during World War II. Covers early black aviation, and the struggles and glories
of the 99th Fighter Squadron which trained near Tuskegee Institute in Alabama.
Includes bibliographical references and index.
1. World War, 1939-1945—Aerial operations, American—Juvenile literature.
2. World War, 1939-1945—Participation, Afro-American—Juvenile literature.
3. Afro-American air pilots—History—Juvenile literature.   4. Tuskegee Army
Air Field (Ala.)—Juvenile literature.   [1. World War, 1939-1945 Aerial operations.   2. World War, 1939-1945—Participation, Afro-American.]   I. Title.
D798.H37   1995   95-14366
940.54'4973—dc20   CIP   AC
ISBN 0-382-39215-9 (JHC)   ISBN 0-382-39217-5 (PBK)

Contents

Acknowledgments

This book is dedicated to the Tuskegee Airmen who, despite the indignity of discrimination and segregation, mastered the flying machine and fought on to glory and medals and commendations, and to those men and women who stood tall against the bigots and said, "You can't steal my ego to make yours bigger. I am as good as you are." I also dedicate this book to my late father, who fought World War II in the South Pacific with his dental drill and medic pack.

Many of those Tuskegee heroes and their relatives helped me. A special thanks to my cousin, Lois Marchbanks, widow of the 332nd's flight surgeon, Vance Marchbanks. She provided a wealth of background material, lots of good advice, and lent some of her special family photos. And a special thanks to Lemuel Custis, my neighbor and a member of the pioneer class, who shared his memories of that remarkable time. I am also indebted to Vernon Haywood and Charles McGee, whom I also interviewed. McGee was also kind enough to entrust me with a number of his treasured photos. Thanks to Doris Brown and James Coleman of the Sacramento chapter of Tuskegee Airmen, Inc., for their assistance with my research. Others who helped were George Watson, Edward Woodward, Robert Matthew, James C. Warren, Tucson's Pima Air Museum, and Ray Martin, my good friend and professional photographer who helped with photo research. And a thank you to someone who was not a Tuskegee Airman but knew a challenging project when he saw one—colleague and fellow author Vincent Marteka, who appointed himself my private clipping service.

BLACK PIONEERS OF
THE CLOUDS

essie Coleman of Chicago got her first view of flying in a World War I newsreel shown in a movie theater. High over a battlefield in France, a small French plane made a sharp dive to the right and, with its machine gun rattling, turned on the German plane following it. The German plane banked to the left with the French plane in pursuit. The year was 1917, fourteen years after the Wright brothers' pioneering 1903 flight from a field in North Carolina.

Bessie Coleman was the second black American licensed pilot.

The idea of being able to fly was new and exciting to most people. But to 21-year-old Bessie Coleman, it was more than that. To fly, to swoop through the air, to climb into the clouds, to dive and turn—that was what she wanted to do. Never mind that blacks were not admitted to flight schools. Never mind that flight instruction cost a lot of money. Bessie Coleman would be a pilot.

Coleman, who worked as a manicurist, began to save money for her goal. She took a second job in a restaurant to earn money for her savings account. If she had the money, surely she could find someone who would teach her to fly.

In 1920, Bessie Coleman got a lucky break. She met Robert Abbott, the publisher of the *Chicago Defender*, a black newspaper. Abbott, through his newspaper, was a

American pilots prepare for a mission over German lines during World War I.

fearless advocate of the rights of black people, attacking segregation, discrimination, and lynching. Abbott knew that the first black American pilot, Eugene Bullard, had learned to fly in France. Bullard had been a member of the famous Lafayette Escadrille, the French-American air squadron that had fought in World War I. Why couldn't Coleman go to France for flight training? In those days, there was little or no discrimination against blacks in France.

Abbott helped Coleman select a French flight school and apply for admission. At Abbott's urging, Coleman took French lessons. In 1921, with her savings as well as money provided by Abbott, Coleman went to France. By 1922, Coleman had earned her pilot's license from the French Federation Aeronautique Internationale.

When she returned home, she was only the second licensed black American pilot.

Coleman's goal now was to teach other blacks to fly. To raise the money for a flight school, Coleman decided to give air shows. Flying was new and exciting. The public was willing to pay to watch pilots put planes through rolls, loops, and dives. Daredevils also performed other feats, such as walking on the plane's wing while another pilot flew the plane. During Labor Day weekend of 1922, Coleman gave her first air show at Curtiss Field near New York City. It was sponsored by Abbott and the *Chicago Defender*. Abbott saw to it that the *Defender* provided a big article about the show. The publicity gave Coleman a chance to spread the word that blacks could aspire to be pilots. Six weeks later Coleman repeated her performance in Chicago at the Checkerboard Airdome (now Midway Airport), again under the sponsorship of Abbott.

Coleman traveled around the country—to Texas, California, and Florida—giving air shows. Her plan was to start a flight school in Los Angeles. In April 1926, she was rehearsing for a show in Jacksonville, Florida. Her earnings from the show would put her over the top, giving her the money she needed for the flight school. But on that April afternoon, Coleman failed to pull her plane out of a dive. She was thrown from the plane and killed.

Coleman's dream of a flight school for blacks did not die with her. William J. Powell, a well-to-do black businessman, had persuaded a white flight school to accept him into its training program. Once he had earned his license, Powell, like Bessie Coleman, wanted to provide that opportunity to other black people. In 1929, he founded the Bessie Coleman Aero Club and School in Los Angeles.

Powell believed that achievement by black pilots would demonstrate black talent and capability and thus lead to decreased segregation and discrimination. To increase black interest in aviation, Powell wrote a book, *Black Wings,* and produced a film, *Unemployment, the Negro, and Aviation.* He also circulated a newsletter, *Craftsmen Aero News,* in the black community. The Bessie Coleman Aero Club gave air shows that featured well-known black and white aviators.

The circuslike atmosphere of air shows excited public interest and involvement in aviation. But serious pilots began to make efforts to show that planes were more than novelties, that they could be used for long-distance transportation of people and freight. With their long-distance flights, white pilots such as Charles Lindbergh and Amelia Earhart showed the way. As black pilots earned their wings, they too began to take part in endurance flying.

On September 18, 1932, black pilot James Banning and his mechanic, Thomas Allen, took off from Los Angeles for Long Island, New York. Most endurance flights were financed by large companies, but Banning and Allen could not find a sponsor. Starting off with $100 for gas and oil, they dubbed themselves the "Flying Hoboes." When they landed for refueling or because of bad weather, Banning and Allen made their way to a black neighborhood, where they usually were given a room and a meal. As they traveled across the country, Banning and Allen attracted the attention of the white press. The 1930s were a time of great unemployment and poverty. The efforts of the two heroes raised the country's spirits. One white newspaper wrote, "It is certainly stimulating that we have heroes who come to light in this very worst of times."

When they ran out of money, Banning and Allen convinced a Texas oil dealer to give them oil and gasoline on credit. In St. Louis, the plane's engine failed. With the help of students at a white trade school, the two took the plane's engine apart and discovered that the valves were worn out. At the suggestion of an instructor, they replaced the valves with those of a 1928 Nash automobile motor. The two were soon back in the air.

In Pittsburgh, Banning and Allen met Robert Vann, a publicity man for presidential candidate Franklin Roosevelt. Vann offered to pay them to throw campaign leaflets from the plane as they flew from Pittsburgh to New York.

Finally, on Sunday, October 9, 1932, three weeks after they had set out, the two landed at Valley Stream Air Feld at Long Island, New York. The trip required 42 hours of air time. Banning and Allen were the first black pilots to make a transcontinental flight. New York welcomed them with a key to the city and a special party at the Cotton Club in Harlem.

In the next two years, the black pilot team of Charles Alfred Anderson and Albert E. Forsythe completed several long-distance flights. In July 1933, they flew from Atlantic City to Los Angeles, then to New York City, then back to the West Coast, landing in San Francisco. They made another flight to Canada that same year.

In 1934, Anderson and Forsythe set out on their Pan-American Goodwill Flight. The pilots named their plane the *Booker T. Washington* in honor of the black educator. The flight began in Miami and made many stops in the Caribbean in places such as Cuba, Jamaica, and Puerto Rico. The mission of the flight was to demonstrate the skill of black pilots and to encourage blacks and whites to get along with each other. It was a mission that the

The public was invited to the christening of the *Booker T. Washington*, an airplane that would be piloted by two black men, Alfred Anderson and Albert Forsythe, on a 1934 goodwill flight.

The 1934 goodwill flight beginning in Miami, Florida would include stops at a number of Caribbean islands.

government of the United States was happy to support. The State Department provided guidance and assistance as the *Booker T. Washington* made its way from island to island. Many of the landing fields had to be improvised; lighting at night was sometimes provided by auto headlights. Everywhere Anderson and Forsythe landed, they were greeted by cheering crowds. Although the adventure ended in Trinidad when the plane was damaged during a takeoff from a dirt runway, the Goodwill Flight received a lot of publicity and made American and Caribbean blacks very proud of the achievement.

As their numbers grew, black pilots founded new flight schools and organizations. In Chicago in 1931, black pilots formed the Challenger Air Pilot Association. In 1933, a second black flight school, the Coffey School of Aeronautics, was founded in Chicago by two pilots, Cornelius Coffey and his wife, Willa Brown. In 1933, also in Chicago, the Negro

Airmen International, Inc. was founded, giving black pilots a national organization of their own. Black pilots were excluded from the all-white Airline Pilots Association.

In 1935, John Robinson, the Challenger Air Pilot Association president, led a group of black pilots and mechanics to Ethiopia. There they intended to help Emperor Haile Selassie build an air force to fight an Italian invasion of his country. But Italy, led by the Fascist dictator Benito Mussolini, overran Ethiopia before Robinson's men could complete their mission. The defeat of Ethiopia by the dictatorial Italian government stimulated black opposition to the wave of fascist conquest sweeping Europe. Both black and white Americans formed the Abraham Lincoln Battalion of the International Brigade, which went to Spain to help fight the takeover there by the Fascist dictator, Francisco Franco. One member of the Brigade was black pilot James Peck. For four months Peck flew air combat missions in the skies over Spain. He shot down five planes, making him an ace. Despite the efforts of the Brigade, the fascists triumphed in Spain.

The defeat of Ethiopia, the fascist victory in Spain, and Nazi Germany's takeover of Austria, Czechoslovakia, and Poland were signposts along the way toward World War II. The major powers—England, France, Germany, Japan, and even the United States—were now building weapons, training armies, and developing new ships and planes. There were about 120 licensed black pilots in the

United States in 1939—living proof that blacks could be pilots. As the war clouds grew thicker, blacks sought to join the armed forces as pilots.

OPENING THE DOOR TO THE AIR CORPS

As World War II approached, anyone in the United States who wanted to be a military pilot had to apply to the U. S. Army or U.S. Navy. The Air Force was not founded until after World War II. Within the Army, there was a small group called the Army Air Service.

Eugene Jacques Bullard learned to fly in France while serving with the French Foreign Legion. He flew as a fighter pilot in a French squadron during World War I.

The Army Air Service had been formed during World War I. At that time, Army generals did not consider airplanes to be a serious weapon of war. Slowly the generals changed their minds about airplanes. But they changed their minds about blacks flying airplanes even more slowly.

In 1914, during the early years of World War I, an American pilot had flown combat missions for France against Germany. France had honored the pilot with its Croix de guerre medal. The skill and knowledge of Eugene Jacques Bullard were just what his country needed in 1917 as it mobilized before entering World War I. But Bullard was black. While other American members of Bullard's squadron, the Franco-American Flying Corps (Lafayette Escadrille), were welcomed into the United States Army Air Service, Bullard was turned away.

Blacks did serve in the United States Army in World War I, some in combat, but most in service units, as kitchen helpers, road builders, stevedores, and grave registrars. Some blacks received officer training and served as officers during the war.

In 1925, the Army Central Staff College (which later became the War College) studied the combat records of black servicemen, with the goal of determining the most efficient way to use blacks in the armed services. The study concluded that black men were cowards and poor technicians and fighters, lacking initiative and resourcefulness. Most of blacks' undesirable qualities were attributed to their being inferior humans with small brains. The study also concluded that blacks' lack of necessary physical, moral, and mental qualities made them unfit to associate with whites. For this reason, concluded the study, blacks should be segregated from whites.

Wrong as these conclusions were, they fit right in with the times. The early 1920s was a very racist time. Many blacks still lived in the South. The states in the southern United States had all sorts of unfair and ridiculous laws designed to keep blacks "down." In the North, segregation in public places degraded blacks. There were plenty of "experts" willing to testify before Congress. Again and again, they testified that not only blacks but also immigrants from Italy, Russia, and Eastern Europe had smaller brains, and no morals, when compared with white Protestants.

Nevertheless, the War College was worried about a manpower shortage. Therefore, despite agreeing with the opinion of the times, the War College recommended that blacks be carefully trained and assigned to segregated combat, engineer, quartermaster, artillery, cavalry, and Air Service units.

In late 1935, Benjamin O. Davis, a black West Point cadet who would graduate 35th in his class of 276 in June 1936, applied to the U.S. Army Air Corps, the successor to the Air Service. Davis's high academic standing entitled him to choose any branch of the army. But a month after he applied, he received a letter denying his admission into the Corps. The response Davis received was similar to the one that all blacks received when applying to the Air Corps. Since the Air Corps had no black units, "there would be no unit to which to assign" him after graduation from flying school. Davis was shocked at the news. He believed the rejection unworthy of America and its ideals. His West Point training had taught him to respect those ideals.

The wording of the rejection letters sent out to blacks applying to the Air Corps throughout the 1930s remained the same as the one sent to Davis. A 1937 follow-up War College study called for admitting more blacks into the army. They would serve in all-black service and combat units but not the Air Corps. The Air Corps said that it required "men of technical and mechanical experience and ability" and noted that "as a rule the colored man has not been attracted to this field in the same way or the same extent as the white man."

In February 1938, the *Pittsburgh Courier*, a black weekly newspaper, launched a campaign to open all armed services to blacks. During that year, nearly every issue of the paper contained articles commenting or reporting on discrimination in the military. Other newspapers and organizations, including the National Association for the Advancement of Colored People (NAACP), joined the effort. The *Courier* began to focus its efforts on the Air Corps, calling for an all-black flying group that would give blacks a chance to prove themselves. The paper covered all Congressional activity dealing with blacks in the Air Corps, commenting in editorials and appealing to readers to write members of Congress.

In April 1939, Congress passed Public Law 18, which authorized the primary training of military pilots by civilian schools. The law was intended to ease the load at the two Air Corps aviation schools, Randolph and Kelly fields in Texas. Senator Harry Schwartz of Wyoming managed to add an amendment to the law that made it apply to blacks. The amendment called for the War Department to lend aviation equipment to at least two schools approved by the Civil Aeronautics Authority (CAA) for training black pilots.

At first it looked as if the Air Corps would be forced to change its policy of black exclusion. But Air Corps officials felt that since the War Department had opposed Senator Schwartz's amendment, the department would not force the Air Corps to comply. The Air Corps issued a statement that rejected the idea of pilot training for blacks.

In June 1939, Congress made another attempt to force the Air Corps's hand. It authorized the CAA

When forced to by Congress, the Army recruited blacks for segregated aviation squadrons. But these men received no technical training.

Civilian Pilot Training Program (CPTP). Twenty thousand college students a year would receive pilot training. The goal was to build up a reserve of civilian pilots who could be called upon to serve as military pilots in case of war. Within three months a black college, West Virginia State, had received CAA approval for a CPTP program. Eventually five other black colleges acquired CPTP programs. Over the next few years, the program produced 400,000 pilots, of whom 2,700 were black. Many blacks scored so well on their exams that they received CAA commendations. Still the Air Corps refused to accept any black CPTP graduates, an outcome predicted by the *Courier* when the program was launched. The paper wrote "The naming of Negro schools where students may receive training as air pilots and mechanics is a step in the right direction, but only a short step. No Negroes have been admitted to the Army Air Corps and there is not the slightest indication at this time that any will be." Keep up the pressure, advised the newspaper.

During 1940, black leaders increased their efforts. In May 1940, Rayford Logan, chairman of the Courier's committee on the Participation of Negroes in the National Defense Program, testified before Congress that the War Department was not complying with the Schwartz amendment to Public Law 18. The War Department asked the Air Corps why it would not accept blacks and received the same reply that black applicants received—no black flying units, no need for black pilots. This response was accepted by the War Department. Privately, Secretary of War Henry Stimson had his doubts about blacks being pilots. In his diary, he wrote that blacks in aviation will "produce disaster there." He doubted the efficiency and initiative of blacks.

In September 1940, Congress passed an amendment to the Selective Training and Services Act that called for the induction, selection, and training of blacks in all military organizations. Shortly thereafter the War Department announced that the Army was complying with the amendment by creating all-black aviation squadrons. But members of these squadrons received no special training and were assigned menial tasks in kitchens, hospitals, and on base grounds. There seemed to be no plans for black pilots. The Air Corps could not envision black officers giving orders to white men. What if a black pilot was forced to land at a white field? No white could be expected to follow his orders to service his plane or provide other needs. Where would he stay and eat? Segregation—separation of blacks and whites—must stand.

Later in 1940, Walter White, secretary of the National Association for the Advancement of Colored People (NAACP); A. Philip Randolph, head of the Brotherhood

Walter White served as secretary of the NAACP from 1931 until his death in 1955.

of Sleeping Car Porters (now part of the Brotherhood of Railway and Airline Clerks); and T. Arnold Hill, a National Urban League representative, met with President Franklin Roosevelt, the secretary of the navy, and the assistant secretary of war to discuss the use of blacks in the armed services. Among the demands of the black leaders was "immediate designation of centers where Negroes may be trained for work in all branches of the aviation corps." They said it was "not enough to train pilots alone, but in addition, navigators, bombardiers, gunners, radiomen, and mechanics must be trained in order to facilitate full Negro participation in the air service." The President listened to the black leaders and made a few suggestions, but no promises.

In 1925, A. Philip Randolph founded the Brotherhood of Sleeping Car Porters, a union he headed until 1968.

In November 1940, the president of Hampton Institute, a black college in Virginia, called a two-day conference at the college to discuss the participation of blacks in national defense. Many black and white leaders attended, including the first lady, Eleanor Roosevelt. The conferees concluded that the Air Corps's refusal to admit blacks as military pilots meant it was breaking a

First Lady Eleanor
Roosevelt was a catalyst
in pushing the Air Force
to desegregate.

law—Public Law 18. The fact that the President's wife was a part of the conference was not lost on the War Department.

In January 1941 the announcement came that blacks could become Air Corps pilots. The War Department announced the formation of an all-black fighter squadron, the 99th Pursuit Squadron. Service personnel for the squadron—those who serviced and armed planes and provided other services to the pilots and planes—would train at Chanute Field, in Rantoul, Illinois. Black Air Corps cadets would receive 15 weeks of primary training—preflight, ground, and flight instruction at Tuskegee Institute in eastern Alabama. Secondary instruction, combat pilot training, would take place at soon-to-be constructed Tuskegee Army Air Field, to be located near the Institute. Once the airfield was built, the cadets would have all their training there.

The Crisis, the NAACP magazine, called the establishment of the 99th Pursuit Squadron "a step in the right direction," but went further, calling for the integration of black people into the armed services. *The Crisis* added that "while the NAACP can be forced to accept" a segregated fighter unit, "we can never agree to it."

Despite the segregated training, the opportunity for blacks was great. A fighter pilot had to fly, navigate, and man the guns all at the same time. To be a fighter pilot was to be very skilled and daring—perhaps the most glamorous job in the military in 1941. The pilot controlled all by himself a machine having tremendous speed and firepower. His job was to attack enemy fighters threatening American bombers as well as targets on the land and sea. Although he was often part of a group, the fighter pilot sometimes engaged in single combat with enemy fighters. Blacks were being given a chance to prove they could handle this challenging assignment.

Tuskegee Institute's pilot training record was one reason the Air Corps chose a site near it for a black military pilot training base. The Institute had made a name for itself in the college-based CPTP program. With the help of federal and state officials, the Institute had secured land for a primary instruction airfield. With materials supplied by the Institute, the students had built Kennedy Field—a hangar, a fuel depot, a restroom building, and a small office. The college's entire CPTP primary aviation class had passed with flying colors, completed their flight test, and received private pilot licenses. Not even one student had "washed out" or failed. Subsequently Tuskegee received CAA authorization for providing secondary flight instruction, the only black college to receive such authorization. Graduates of primary training at other black colleges came to Tuskegee for secondary training. Tuskegee's chief aviation instructor was Charles Anderson, the pioneer pilot who made transcontinental flights in 1933 and 1934.

Shortly after its announcement, the Air Corps began to put its plan into action. Orders went out. The construction of Tuskegee Army Air Field began. Applications were processed. The Tuskegee Experiment, as the Air Corps called it, was about to begin—testing whether blacks had the skill, intellect, and courage to be military pilots.

Chapter Three

TRYING THEIR WINGS

*T*he eyes of your country and the eyes of your people
are upon you. The success of the venture depends
upon you.

On the campus of
Alabama's Tuskegee
Institute, class 42C, the
first black Army Air
Cadet pilots, attends
ceremonies initiating
black military aviation.
Behind the speaker's
platform can be seen
a statue of Booker
T. Washington, first
president of Tuskegee.

The speaker was Major General Walter Weaver, commander of the U.S. Army's Southeastern Air Corps
Training Command. The date was July 19, 1941. The
place was the Tuskegee Institute campus near a statue of
Booker T. Washington, Tuskegee's first president.
Weaver's words were directed to the 13 young black men
who formed the first class of black pilot trainees—class
42C. The trainees were mostly college graduates, includ-

ing a policeman, an army officer, a factory inspector, and several young men who were fresh out of college.

All but one member of class 42C wore crisp khaki. Lemuel Custis, traveling from Hartford, Connecticut, had just arrived that morning. "I was traveling at the direction of Uncle Sam," he said, "and there was no time to get a uniform before the ceremony. I remember I had on a brown gabardine suit." Custis remembered his feelings during the ceremony: "We were enthused because we felt that at last we had a great opportunity in the Air Corps. We were happy to be there. It was a proud feeling. We were focused on the task—didn't feel like pioneers or anything. Later, looking back, we realized our trailbreaking role."

During the ceremony, congratulatory telegrams from Army Chief of Staff General George Marshall and Air Corps Chief General Henry (Hap) Arnold were read. Despite all the speeches and telegrams, many Air Corps officers viewed the program with suspicion or amusement. General Weaver privately told the Tuskegee Airmen training officer not to worry about standards. "Just keep 'em happy," he said. A member of Weaver's staff had grave doubts about the program. He believed that contributing to the power of blacks would probably fuel a world war between blacks and whites. But he said, "We just do our job."

Despite such private doubts, the Air Corps proceeded to provide blacks with the same kind of aviation facilities and training provided to whites.

This is what the pilots saw as they neared Tuskegee Army Air Field.

A few miles away from the Tuskegee campus, black contractors were building temporary Moton Field, which would be used for primary training—simple take-offs and landings—of the new cadets. At another site, Tuskegee Army Air Field (TAAF) was being built. Here the first class of black cadets would receive most of their training. Once the base was built future classes of black cadets would receive primary and all other training there.

TAAF would be a full-fledged Air Corps base—headquarters and offices, runways, barracks, mess halls, officers club, warehouses, hospital, hangars, theater, and post exchange. Once complete, the base would be able to train 33 fighter pilots at once. Fourteen training aircraft would form the first flight line—planes available to fly. Later, as more and more trainees poured in, new runways would be built and the flight line would grow to more than 50 planes.

Located six miles away from the Institute and the TAAF site was the town of Tuskegee, Alabama. The atmosphere in the town was hostile to blacks. The local sheriff was especially cruel. Strict segregation and discrimination made it difficult or impossible to buy food or clothing in the stores. Restaurants and the one movie theater provided segregated areas for blacks. Little or no housing was available in the town for black civilian instructors and base employees who were ineligible for housing at TAAF. When the citizens of Tuskegee learned that a black airfield was going up near their town, they wrote letters, signed petitions, and contacted their senators. When this did no good, the people of Tuskegee charged that the new airfield would block expansion of the town. When it was noted that the new airfield was to be over six miles away, the complaint was dropped. Some whites in those days feared

Standing at attention in front of their training planes, the first class of Tuskegee cadets salute Major James A. Ellison, their base commander.

what they believed to be the menace of a large group of blacks being trained to wage war.

For the most part, black Air Corps personnel kept to themselves at TAAF, which offered everything needed for comfort and entertainment. Celebrities such as Louis Armstrong, Lena Horne, Joe Louis, and the Camel Caravan orchestra entertained the troops, as did opera singers Grace Moore and Richard Crooks. The base sponsored personnel sports teams, a glee club, orchestras, and art exhibits.

The Air Corps assigned white officers to command TAAF. Major James Ellison, the first commanding officer, oversaw the establishment of TAAF. Ellison was a strong supporter of black military aviation. He had joined the president of Tuskegee on a trip to Washington to urge the War Department to establish the airfield at Tuskegee. His ambition, he often said, was to fly across the country with a black squadron to prove to the nation that blacks could be pilots.

Major Noel Parrish commanded the training program. Before reporting to his new assignment, Parrish met with anthropology professors at the University of Chicago to discuss their opinions about race. As he assumed his duties and acquired black friends, Parrish came to despise racial segregation. As training officer, he often had to answer questions from curious white people: "How do Negroes fly?" "Are blacks better fliers because they're closer to nature?" "Are those really Negroes up there or are you doing it for them?"

Parrish's training for the 13 members of class 42C began promptly after the Institute's opening ceremony on that July day in 1941. Before they could earn their wings, the cadets would have to complete three phases of train-ing—primary, basic, and advanced. In primary and basic, they would have ground school classroom courses and flying lessons. In advanced, the cadets would concentrate on mil-itary flying. For a while, classrooms for primary ground school were set up in a dormitory on the Tuskegee campus. There the cadets studied the basic science and engi-neering they would need in order to be pilots. Aeronautics taught them what makes a plane fly. They learned about the weather, what condi-tions produce wind and rain, and the effect of weather conditions on the flight of the plane. They learned to read aviation maps and to navigate.

Lieutenants T. A. Wilson and Wylie Seldon (in the cockpit) study the con-trols of the P-40 fighter plane, the plane they will fly in combat.

In August, primary flying lessons at Moton Field began. The cadets learned the maneuvers that changed the plane's direction, speed, and altitude. The key was using the controls—"the stick" or control column and the foot pedals—to move panels located on the plane's wings and tail section. Moving the panels (elevators) on the tail section cause the plane to takeoff and climb or descend and land. Flaps, which are located along the trailing rear edges of the wings, add to the lift created by the wing and allow planes to takeoff and land at safer speeds. Helping the airplane turn and maneuver in the air are the ailerons—located on the outer edges of the wings—and the rudder, located on the vertical portion of the tail section.

Pioneering Tuskegee Army Air Field class 42C graduates listen carefully to their instructor. Standing, left to right, Instructor: Lt. Robert M. Long, George S. Roberts; Capt. Benjamin O. Davis, Jr., Charles DeBow, Mac Ross, and Lemuel R. Custis.

The cadet flew with an instructor in the back seat, who gave instructions and watched carefully to see how the instructions were carried out. The instructor showed the student how to land if the engine failed. With the instructor on board, the cadet practiced takeoffs, landings, and other maneuvers. After about eight hours of instruction, the cadet was expected to solo—to take the plane up, fly it, and land it by himself.

"Soloing was a good feeling. I knew it was only the first tiny step in the journey toward getting those wings. But it was a big deal," said Lemuel Custis.

Custis found that the hardest part of training was satisfying the instructors. "They were watching—evaluating our skills as a pilot, observing the way we maneuvered the plane, navigated. They had the final say," he said.

If a cadet was not measuring up, he was called into the instructor's office. Said Custis, who eventually became a flight instructor, "Instructors can sense that a person simply lacks the aptitude to fly. If they had decided you weren't measuring up, they'd tell you in a minute—'You're not going to kill yourself and me in the aircraft. Mister you're out, washed out.'" The next day that cadet stayed in the barracks. Within a few days, he was gone. "They told us all on the day we began training, 'Look to your left, look to your right. Those men won't make it.' That turned out to be about right," said Custis. Only Custis and five of his classmates, out of a class of

Instructor Lieutenant Donald McPherson explains a cross-country aviation map to a group of Tuskegee Air Cadets.

thirteen, moved on to basic training at TAAF. Shortly afterward, one more washed out. In basic they flew bigger planes, learned to fly in formation, and took more advanced ground classes.

Left to right: Lt. John Daniels, Cadets Clayborne Lockett, Lawrence Clark, William Melton, and civilian instructor, Milton Crenshaw, plan the route for a night flying exercise.

On December 7, 1941, in the midst of class 42C's training, the Japanese bombed the U.S. Navy base at Pearl Harbor, Hawaii. The next day, the United States declared war, joining the Allies— Great Britain, France, and Russia—in the fight against the Axis powers—Germany, Italy, and Japan.

In advanced training, cadets honed their flying skills. They practiced forced landings, loops, slow rolls, and steep climbing turns called chandelles. They learned night flying. At that time, TAAF didn't have the equipment for night flying—landing lights and other signaling equipment. In the late afternoon, the cadets would travel in jeeps to Maxwell Field near Montgomery for night flying. Before they took off, they would plot their course, making note of what time they should pass certain landmarks. These landmarks included towns lit by street lights, highways lit by the headlights of moving cars, and beacons atop towers blinking their location in code.

Once the cadets had learned to fly, it was time to learn to be fighter pilots, and to receive gunnery training. They learned how to strafe—fly low and blast away at targets on the ground. Aircraft towed banners that provided targets for shooting in the sky.

Finally the training was over. Class 42C had mastered all the skills needed to be fighter pilots. On March 7, 1942, five men marched onto TAAF runway for graduation. They received their certificates of course completion. Orders were read promoting Lemuel Custis, Mac Ross, George Roberts, and Charles DeBow to the rank of second lieutenant in the Army Air Force. (That month the Army Air Corps had become the Army Air Force.) The fifth member of Class 42C was Army Captain Benjamin O. Davis, Jr., the West Point graduate who had attempted to become a pilot in 1935. Davis became an Air Force captain. The new Army Air Force officers took

Pilots celebrate with their families after graduation at the TAAF base chapel in the background. As graduate pilots, they had earned the right to remove the stiff grommels from the crowns of their hats, giving the hats the "crushed" dashing look of a pilot.

the oath of office. Then their wives and mothers pinned silver wings on the pilots' khaki blouses. The wings told the world that these men were pilots. The Army Air Force now included five black fighter pilots.

If they did not realize that they had made history, the Army chief of air staff, General George Stratemeyer, was there to remind them: "The vast unseen audience of your well-wishers senses that this graduation is an historic moment. . . . Future graduates of this school will look up to you as Old Pilots. They will be influenced profoundly by the examples you set."

Even as the five looked ahead to combat, other cadets were following in their footsteps—through primary, basic, and advanced training. As each class graduated, the pilots were assigned to the 99th Fighter Squadron, the all-black squadron activated by the Air Force. (Three squadrons form a group, but the 99th, as yet, had no group assignment.) Soon there would enough pilots to fill the 99th. Looking ahead to the day when there would be enough fliers to man a second squadron, the Air Force activated the 100th Fighter Squadron in May 1942. Lieutenant Mac Ross, one of the pioneering graduates was appointed commander of the 100th. Benjamin O. Davis, Jr., who by had been promoted to lieutenant colonel, was named commanding officer of the 99th.

July 3, 1942, was graduation day for the fourth class. These men would fill the last openings needed to bring the 99th up to its full strength of 26 pilots. Davis was

Black Air Corps pilots report to the flight line.

the graduation speaker. He saluted the graduates' success in proving, to the surprise of many, that blacks could meet Air Force standards for military pilots. Tuskegee has done its job, he said, "Now we must do ours in the air against the enemy."

Joining the pilots in the 99th were 14 other officers, who provided support services and commanded the 35 enlisted men who serviced the planes. The enlisted men had trained at Chanute Field, in Rantoul, Illinois. In nine months to a year, they had mastered skills the Air Force said should require at least five years.

The 99th was proud and ready for combat. Their country was at war, and they wanted to join the fight.

The pilots perfected their fighter skills in the P-40, the plane they would fly in combat. The plane's long nose and low seat reduced visibility while taxiing. The P-40 was slower than they had expected but very maneuverable. They honed their navigational skills. The pilots became so accurate at hitting gunnery targets that headquarters banned them from practice during certain hours to preserve the targets for other pilots. Ground crews sharpened their skills, changing plane engines in one-third the time required. Pilots practiced formation flying, becoming so good that the 99th earned Air Force commendations for precision flying. In October 1942 the inspecting general of the Third Air Force called the 99th "in excellent condition and ready for immediate departure overseas."

As they marched the streets of TAAF at 120 steps a minute, the members of the 99th chanted their fight song:

Fight! Fight! Fight! Fight—Fight—Fight!
The fighting Ninety-Ninth!
We are the heroes of the night
To hell with Axis might!

Rat-tat! Rat-tat-tat!
Round in planes we go
When we fly, Ninety-Ninth
This is how we go.

Cadets in training watched as the 99th flashed by, admiring their skill and yearning to join them to fly and fight.

The 99th was ready, but no combat orders came. The Air Force couldn't decide where to send the squadron. Originally the Air Force had planned to send the 99th to Liberia to fight the Germans on the African front. But by the fall of 1942, the Allies were winning in Africa. Then it was decided to send the squadron to India and Burma. For some reason this was abandoned. Then the Allies began making plans to move from Africa north to Sicily. The Allies decided to deploy large numbers of troops to the Sicilian campaign. The 99th was to be one of those units. But exactly when and where they would go had yet to be decided.

In the meantime, as they waited, the morale of the 99th dropped. Colonel Frederick von Kimble, the new base commander, had filled TAAF with "colored" and "white" signs on the restrooms, drinking fountains, and other sites on the base. This was segregation within an already segregated base and it was profoundly depressing to the black personnel. Many northern blacks were not used to "colored water and white water." Then in early 1943, Kimble left and Colonel Noel Parrish, the training officer, was made base commander. The "colored" and "white" signs came down, and blacks felt they had a friend in the commandant's office. But still no orders came for the 99th. The men began to fear they would never get to put their skills to work in the service of their country. Constantly they were put on standby alert—all leaves canceled, everyone confined to base. Were they finally going? Then the alert would suddenly be canceled.

As they waited and wondered, the 99th added to the crowded situation at the base. The Air Force considered TAAF its single base for all black personnel. There were classes of cadet pilots, training to man the 100th Fighter Squadron and the two other squadrons, the 301st and the 302nd, which would make up the 332nd Fighter Group. Black nonflying officers fresh out of Officer Candidate School poured in. Black Signal Corps cadets, an ordnance company, and several service units were assigned to TAAF. By mid-1942 approximately 217 officers and 3,000 enlisted men had been assigned to the base.

By early 1943, officials in Washington were starting to ask why the 99th had still not gone into combat, nearly seven months after finishing training. William Hastie, a black civilian aide to the secretary of war, resigned in protest against Air Force policies. Several weeks later he released a pamphlet titled *On Clipped Wings.* In it he charged that "by not wanting the Negro in the first place and by doubting his capacity, the Air Command has committed itself psychologically to . . . actions which become major obstacles to the success of Negroes in the Air Force."

First Lady Eleanor Roosevelt wrote to the Air Force, asking why black pilots were not being sent into combat. "Does this mean that none of those trained are being used in active service?" she asked.

Secretary of War Henry Stimson visited the base. After inspecting the 99th and talking to Colonel Parrish, Stimson—the man who felt blacks could never become pilots—became a believer. He pronounced the 99th "outstanding by any standard."

Soon the 99th saw signs that something was about to happen. Training was intensified. Pilots practiced combat flying, formation flying, and night flying. The entire squadron was led on 25-mile hikes and taught the fundamentals of setting up a campsite and running it.

Pilots were taught to use radar, a new technology. They learned to track other planes, guide the mission, and bring the planes home. "Pay attention," they were told. "Where you're going, you'll be alone."

Colonel Noel Parrish, Tuskegee Army Air Field commander.

Finally on April 1, 1943, over a year after graduation of the first class, the word came—"Moving out." On that day the pilots filled the skies over TAAF with last-minute practicing—low-altitude flybys, formations, and graceful arching climbs into the sky. It was their way of saying good-bye.

Colonel Parrish, who had always believed in the 99th, said good-bye too. "You are fighting men now. You have made the team. Your future is now being handed into your own hands. Your future, good or bad, will depend largely on how determined you are not to give satisfaction to those who would like to see you fail."

On April 2, the 99th climbed aboard a train that would take them to New York, where they would board a troop ship. Hundreds of well-wishers came to the tiny Tuskegee train station to say good-bye.

Chapter Four

THE 99TH GOES TO WAR

The *S.S. Mariposa* had been a shiny white luxury liner, carrying travelers to Hawaii and other vacation spots. But like many other passenger ships during World War II, the *Mariposa* had been painted a dull gray camouflage color and pressed into service as a troop ship. The ship, docked in Brooklyn, would carry the 99th into battle.

The order to board came on April 15, 1943. The 400 members of the 99th joined 3,500 white servicemen boarding the *Mariposa*. The officer in charge of those 3,900 troops while on board was Lieutenant Colonel Benjamin O. Davis, Jr., the 99th squadron commander. As onboard troop commander, Davis and his staff from the 99th supervised all of the activities of the troops traveling into battle, including mess, discipline, and daily schedule. Davis felt highly honored to carry out this assignment. At last, after training at segregated Tuskegee Army Air Field, Davis and the 99th felt that they were an important part of the war effort. Davis was proud of his squadron. Its officers, wearing the silver wings of pilots, drew the admiration of the other troops. As the ship left the pier, Davis felt that he and his men were leaving racial discrimination behind. He hoped for more "freedom and respect" for his men than they had enjoyed at home.

But as the ship prepared for sailing, Captain Elmer Jones, who was in charge of the 99th Service Detachment, was distressed when he learned that a great deal of the equipment his men needed was not on board.

His detachment was charged with providing aircraft supplies and services such as major repair of the planes. They were also to assist the 99th ground crew with the repair of engines, radios, and other instruments. Jones had been promised the equipment upon the *Mariposa's* departure. When it did not arrive, Jones was told to expect it at his destination. Now he looked anxiously at the horizon, hoping to find it at the end of the voyage.

The destination turned out to be Casablanca, Morocco, in North Africa, where the *Mariposa* docked on April 24, 1943. From there, the 99th traveled in trucks to their training base, Oued N'ja, near the town of Fez, in Morocco.

At Oued N'ja the 99th found a bare dirt strip. It was up to them to make the base a place where they could live and work. The troops pitched tents but slept on the ground for awhile until their cots arrived. The men dug slit trenches to use as bathrooms, but there were no tarpaulins to cover them. The cooks prepared meals from the contents of mess kits. Local Arab women were recruited to do the laundry.

Ferry pilots picked up brand-new P-40 Warhawks at Casablanca and delivered them to the 99th at Oued N'ja. The pilots were delighted to have new planes, as all of their training planes had been used and old. They put the new planes through their paces from the hard-packed dirt runways.

But Captain Jones found that the service equipment he needed had not met the 99th at its destination. As it turned out, Jones did not see the materials for nearly eight months. "In spite of these obstacles, the detachment went right to work for the 99th with the resources at hand," he said. "At Oued N'ja, the detachment made the 99th's first overseas engine change."

For a month, the pilots trained for combat. They practiced dogfights with the fighter pilots of the 27th Fighter Group, which was stationed at a large American base nearby. Said Lieutenant Colonel Davis, "It was a serious game; each side tried to demonstrate superior flying ability by getting on the tail of the opponent in a position to fire."

Normally a few combat-experienced pilots would be assigned to a squadron that was going into combat for the first time. These experienced pilots would guide and advise the inexperienced ones. But 1943 was a time of segregation. No white pilot could be assigned to the black 99th, and no black pilots had seen combat yet. But at their practice base at Oued N'ja, the pilots of the 99th got advice and guidance from three experienced white pilots. One was Colonel Philip Cochran, who was so famous that he became the model for the cartoon character Flip Corkin in Milton Caniff's comic strip *Terry and the Pirates.*

After about a month of training, the 99th moved east from Morocco to Tunisia. Their combat base was at Fardjouna, near the city of Tunis on Africa's northern coast. Their duty as fighter pilots was to escort bombers and ship convoys, protecting them from enemy fighter planes. The pilots were also assigned dive-bombing missions—diving low, dropping bombs on a target, and swooping away. Another part of their mission was strafing—flying low and machine-gunning ground targets such as bridges and truck convoys.

The 99th had moved into an area where the air war had practically been won. The Allies had cleared the Germans out of North Africa, and Allied planes dominated the skies. The pilots of the 99th soon discovered that there were few enemy aircraft to fight. They found themselves based in North Africa and fighting on the fringes of the Sicilian campaign to the north.

At Fardjouna, Lieutenant Colonel Davis reported to Colonel William Momyer, commanding officer of the white 33rd Fighter Group, to which the 99th was attached. At the base where the 33rd had been stationed for several months, the men of the 99th got their first look at the results of war. Planes with wings torn by bullets and antiaircraft fire limped into base—some nearly torn apart. The men of the 99th saw pilots die. They saw the faces of pilots and ground crewmen when a plane did not return.

In early June 1943, the 99th pilots went into combat. Their first mission was to strafe the Italian island of Pantelleria. Each day for a week, planes of the 99th went out, strafing and sometimes dive-bombing gun positions identified by their intelligence officer. Not a single enemy fighter opposed them. It seemed more like training practice than warfare.

On June 9, the 99th got its first real taste of combat. The squadron was on a bomber escort mission to Pantelleria. As they prepared to escort the bombers home, the pilots spotted a group of German fighters. Part of the squadron escorted the bombers home. The others—lieutenants Charles Dryden, Leon Roberts, Leon Rayford, Spann Watson, and Willie Ashley—went after the enemy planes, climbing to get ready to attack. Roberts saw the German planes diving from the direction of the sun, bearing down on them at 450 miles per hour. He veered away to escape. The rest of the group followed.

Dryden climbed far above the enemy planes and then dove, spraying the tails of the enemy with bullets. Two enemy planes ganged up on Rayford, one damaging his right wing, but he fought back. Just when the Germans were about to finish Rayford off, Watson managed to hit one of the enemy planes. At this point the two German planes retreated. Meanwhile Ashley, who had gone into a spin after the first scramble away from the enemy, found himself near another plane. Assuming the plane was friendly, he drew closer, but when he realized the plane was an enemy, Ashley attacked it. The enemy plane began to smoke and lose altitude. As Ashley followed the falling enemy plane, antiaircraft fire forced him to turn back.

All the planes of the 99th returned safely. The pilots had met the test for that day. They had learned that a person could be trained to fly a plane and shoot the guns, but only combat could teach attack skills. The fighter pilot had to believe he could kill and that he could escape when he got in trouble. Having this offensive spirit enabled the pilot to attack instantly and successfully. Without that spirit and confidence, the pilot eventually could be shot down.

The pilots had also learned something about their P-40s. Most of the enemy fighters could fly higher and faster than the 99th could. Thus the enemy pilots could choose the time and place of a battle, diving from high altitudes, at high speed, out of the sun, surprising Allied fighters. The pilots of the 99th learned to keep watch as they flew, looking up and to the sides and the rear.

Pantelleria surrendered on June 11—the first enemy territory defeated by air power alone. In the following days, the islands of Lampeduca and Limosa also surrendered. Now the Allies had complete control of the seas leading to the large Italian island of Sicily and to mainland Italy.

The Allies began to focus on Sicily. The 99th's role now was to escort bombers on missions to Sicily. On July 2, during a bomber escort mission over southwest Sicily, 99th pilot Lieutenant Charles Hall spotted a group of enemy fighters following enemy bombers. It was his eighth mission and the first time he had seen an enemy plane close up. Hall spotted the fighters following the bombers just after the bomb drop. He moved into the space between the bombers and the enemy fighters, turned on the German formation, and began firing. He saw his bullets enter one of the planes, which rolled sideways and plunged to the ground. Hall followed the enemy plane and saw it crash in a cloud of dust, confirming that he indeed shot it down.

Hall put his plane into a victory roll as he flew over the base. Everyone on the ground knew that a 99th pilot had shot down an enemy plane—the first for the squadron. The men cheered and flashed the *V* for victory as Hall landed. But as the ground crew counted the returning planes, the cheers turned to silence. Two pilots—lieutenants Sherman White and James McCullin—had not returned. Later the 99th learned that the two had been killed in a midair collision.

As Hall's plane rolled to a stop on the field, he was surrounded by men who wanted to know all the details. They also had a surprise for him. While moving up to Fardjouna, they had stopped at a large air base at Tunis, where someone bought a bottle of Coca-Cola. This bottle of the popular soft drink, probably the only one in the Mediterranean combat zone, had been placed in the squadron safe, waiting to be given to the first man to shoot down an enemy plane. The drink was iced and handed to Hall as he hopped onto the landing field. Later Hall was awarded the Distinguished Flying Cross.

For the next week, the 99th helped keep the pressure on Sicily—escorting bombers, strafing enemy airfields, and divebombing enemy supply warehouses, highways, and telephone and radio center. On July 10 the 99th escorted Allied ships sailing from North Africa to invade

Sicily. By July 14, the Allies commanded enough of Sicily that it was safe to set up their own airfields.

On July 19 the 33rd Fighter Group, including the 99th Fighter Squadron, moved from its North African base to Licata on the southern coast of Sicily. From Licata, the 99th joined in the Sicilian campaign, sometimes flying as many as 13 missions a day. Such a schedule was brutal for the pilots, it was also hard on the ground crews, who had to service and arm the planes as they returned. The Sicilian campaign continued throughout July and August until the last of the enemy forces were defeated.

In early September, Lieutenant Colonel Davis was ordered to

The 99th's landing field at Licata, Sicily. Pilots flying P-40s are taking off for patrol missions.

return to the United States to take command of the 332nd Fighter Group. This group was made up of three squadrons of Tuskegee Airmen—the 100th, 301st, and the 302nd. Captain George Roberts was named as the new squadron commander of the 99th.

With Sicily defeated, the Allies' attention turned to mainland Italy where the plan was to invade Salerno, on Italy's southwestern coast, and take over enough of the surrounding countryside to make it possible to set up airfields. Planes operating from these bases could then attack Germany.

The 33rd and the 99th were unable to provide air support for the Salerno invasion because their P-40s had too short a range to fly the round-trip distance from the base to the invasion beach. Thus for the first ten days of September, while the Salerno invasion was taking place, the 33rd and the 99th were more or less idle. As planned, the engineers completed airfield runways near Paestum, just south of Salerno, on September 11. On that day, one officer and 78 service personnel from the 99th flew to the Paestum base to prepare for the arrival of the planes. On September 13 and 14, the three white squadrons of the 33rd Fighter Group flew into Paestum. The 99th Squadron was ordered to remain at the base in southern Sicily.

Then the Germans launched a swift, desperate counteroffensive, driving the Allied invaders back toward the Salerno beach. The Allies ordered every available man and plane into the battle to fight the Germans. The service personnel of the 99th at the Paestum base were issued guns. The white pilots of the 33rd were ordered into the air and, within a few days, they shot down 11 enemy planes.

Thus the 99th had missed the big Paestum battle. Not until September 23 were 10 of the 99th's pilots and planes ordered to Paestum. The rest of the squadron remained in Sicily, too far from the Italian campaign to take part.

Why was the 99th left behind the battle lines and out

of the war? The reason may have had something to do with events back in the United States, where the 99th was undergoing attack by its own commanders. The matter had begun when the 33rd Fighter Group's commander, Colonel Momyer, wrote a negative report about the 99th's performance. This report slowly worked its way up the Air Force chain of command. Although they had no direct knowledge of the 99th, each level of command added negative comments of its own. Finally, bristling with negative comments, the report reached the chief of the Air Force, General Henry "Hap" Arnold, who sent it on to the McCloy Committee of the War Department.

The McCloy Committee's job was to make policy on the use of black troops. Now it was presented with a report from the highest levels of the Air Force, stating, "the 99th was not aggressive, did not have the will to win or reach an objective, did not have the needed stamina, and could not fight as a team," and recommended that all black squadrons be assigned noncombat roles.

This report greeted Lieutenant Colonel Davis when he arrived back in the United States to assume his new command. Davis was furious. Most of Momyer's charges referred to the inexperienced squadron's first few days in combat. Davis felt that Momyer's report reflected Air Force racism—the belief that blacks lacked the innate ability to be fighter pilots.

On October 16, Davis was ordered to testify before the McCloy Committee. In his testimony, Davis pointed out the 99th squadron's lack of combat experience. In the first days of combat, the unit certainly had made mistakes resulting from inexperience. But these mistakes were quickly corrected and the report said nothing about that. Addressing the question of stamina, Davis pointed out that the 99th had operated continuously for two months without receiving replacement pilots. During that time, pilots often flew three to six missions a day, day in and day out.

The Air Force and the War Department continued to doubt that blacks could be successful combat pilots. Nevertheless, they decided to send the three squadrons of the 332nd Fighter Group overseas to join the 99th combat. But apparently, Davis's testimony did cause the Army to seek more information about the 99th. The Army ordered a study entitled "Operations of the 99th Fighter Squadron Compared With Other P-40 Squadrons in the Mediterranean Theater of Operations." The results of the study would settle the matter of black capability as combat pilots. The study was to cover July 1943 through February 1944 and would rate the 99th with respect to missions, readiness, enemy losses, and squadron losses.

While Davis was fighting the 99th's stateside enemies, the squadron continued to battle its country's enemies. On October 17, 1943, the day after Davis's testimony, the 99th was ordered to Foggia Air Field on Italy's eastern coast, where it was attached to the 79th Fighter Group. The 79th was commanded by Colonel Earl Bates, who proved to be a very fair leader. Contrary to Air Force practice, Bates integrated the planes of his group, assigning 79th pilots to fly with those of the 99th, and 99th pilots to fly with those of the 79th. The 79th was experienced in combat. The 99th, which had been flying mostly beach patrol missions since July, had not encountered enemy aircraft for three months. As a result, the 99th pilots still had little aerial combat experience. As they flew bombing and strafing missions with the 79th pilots, the 99th pilots learned better combat takeoff techniques, flight maneuvers, and combat formations. They learned how to pursue the enemy, when to shoot, and what to aim for. The black pilots were gaining experience—and from that came confidence.

In November, the 99th encountered a new enemy— rain and mud. The bad weather often grounded the planes. Winds blew down the unit's tents. The 99th spent most of its time on the ground trying to keep warm and out of the mud. December was no better, and morale was low. Since June the pilots had flown 255 missions but had shot down only one enemy plane. Even their own ground crews were beginning to lose faith in the pilots.

In mid-January 1944, the 79th and the 99th moved to Capodichino Airfield, near Naples on the western coast of Italy. From there, the squadrons supported the terrible battle of Anzio, just south of Rome. The three squadrons of the 79th patrolled the assault beaches at Anzio, preventing the enemy from bringing in more troops and supplies. The 99th guarded the Allied ship convoys carrying troops and supplies to the Anzio beachhead.

On January 27, a 99th flight spotted a group of German fighter planes attacking the ships near the beach. The 99th pilots attacked. Lieutenants Howard Baugh and Clarence Allen destroyed one enemy plane. Lieutenant Willie Ashley chased another, shooting as he went, finally destroying the enemy plane. Lieutenant Leon Roberts chased another at low altitude, shooting at the plane until it crashed into the ground. Lieutenant Robert Diez shot down another, while Lieutenant Henry Perry fired his guns at an enemy plane coming out of a dive, sending it wing-first to earth.

As the 99th ground crews watched their planes returning, they could not believe their eyes. Five victory rolls? Could it be? There was much cheering and backslapping as the pilots landed.

That afternoon another 99th beach patrol scored more victories. Captain Lemuel Custis and lieutenants Charles Bailey and Wilson Eagleson shot down three more enemy planes. Lieutenant Samuel Bruce, who had last been seen chasing two German planes, was lost in the battle. During the battle, Major Roberts, the squadron commander, took a serious hit that damaged his plane's right electrical system and right side guns. As he limped back to base, Roberts spotted an enemy machine gun nest. With his remaining left side guns, Roberts destroyed the gun position.

The next day, Diez and Lieutenant Lewis Smith each shot down an enemy plane. Lieutenant Charles Hall, who had scored the 99th's first aerial victory, gunned down two more. In two days, pilots of the 99th chalked up 12 enemy planes destroyed, three probables, and four damaged. (Someone had to see a plane actually crash before it could be considered destroyed. A badly damaged plane heading downward was considered a probable.) The next day, Major General John Cannon, one of the officers who had endorsed the negative report made against the 99th flew in to congratulate the 99th. "Keep shooting," he said as he left. And they did.

January, 1944: Men of the 99th Fighter Squadron, stationed near Naples, Italy, talk over the day's triumphs during which they shot down eight enemy planes. Lieutenant Leon Roberts (standing, left) remembered chasing one plane at low altitude almost all the way to Rome before he shot it down.

While on beach patrol on February 5, Lieutenant Elwood Driver shot down an enemy plane. Two days later lieutenants Eagleson, Leonard Jackson, and Clinton Mills got three more.

During the rest of February and March, the squadron supported the battle to take Monte Cassino, a German-fortified monastery atop a mountain. As part of Operation Strangle, a supply destruction mission, the 99th divebombed and strafed German rail and shipping supply lines between the Po River Valley in central Italy and the front near the coast. Operation Strangle was so successful that the Germans were forced to truck supplies around broken bridges at night.

Arriving in combat during World War II, the Tuskegee Airmen were based in Tunisia, later moving to Sicily and then to the western and eastern coasts of Italy. From Italy, they flew missions against the Germans over most of Europe.

The Mediterranean and European Theaters of World War I

When the weather kept the pilots on the ground, there was still much to do. Pilots tested and adjusted plane engines. New pilots were combat trained. Official cross-country trips were made. Ground crews, with all the planes at their disposal, overhauled engines, cleaned and calibrated guns, and repaired fuselages and wings. Ground crews sometimes lacked the parts they needed, so they would hop in a jeep and drive to a supply depot or another base to find the needed parts. They begged, borrowed, and sometime salvaged parts from wrecked planes.

News came in April that the 99th was to be separated from the 79th and moved to another base, where it would be attached to another squadron. The 99th gave a farewell party in downtown Naples. There black and white pilots celebrated together their six months of teamwork and comradeship.

April also brought news of the Army's statistical study of the 99th. The study covered the record of the 99th from July 1943 to February 1944. "An examination of the record of the 99th Fighter Squadron reveals no significant general differences between this squadron and the balance of the P-40 squadrons in the Mediterranean theater of operations," said the opening statement of the report. It went on to point out that the squadron had performed well in all three of its fighter pilot roles—divebombing, strafing, and bomber escort. The 99th was recognized as a "superb tactical fighter unit."

Chapter Five

THREE MORE
SQUADRONS GO TO WAR

The three squadrons making up the 332nd Fighter Group—the 100th, 301st, and 302nd—arrived in Italy early in February 1944. The group settled in at Montecorvino Air Base, on Italy's west coast just south of Naples. The pilots then took delivery of their combat planes, P-39 Aircobras. Like the P-40s used by the 99th, the P-39 was slower than the German fighters. The cockpit was smaller, so that a six-footer had to bend down over the controls. However the P-39 was armed with more powerful guns than the P-40.

The 332nd's first assignment was to patrol Italy's western coast, protecting convoys and the Anzio harbor. For three months, the squadrons saw little or no action. Enemy planes were sighted three times, but the pilots found that their P-39s were too slow to catch the Germans. One pilot said of a fleeing German pilot, "He just walked away from us."

But a new assignment and faster planes were in the 332nd's future, because General Ira Eaker, commander of the 15th Air Force, had a problem. The general had been sending bombers to destroy German supply lines and factory centers in northern France and Germany. But since the bombers had no fighter escorts, many were being lost to enemy fighters. Eaker was unable to get enough fighter commanders to agree to fly escort for the bombers. Some commanders argued that the bombers would get all the credit for victory in the air war. Others argued that since the fighters could not carry enough fuel to escort the bombers all the way to the target, they

would not be able to protect them in the most danger-
ous area, near the target. When Eaker equipped fighter
planes with extra fuel tanks, pilots refused to fly with
them because the heavy tanks affected the maneuver-
ability of the planes.

In a meeting, Eaker described his problem to
Lieutenant Colonel Davis, noting that he had lost 114
bombers in February.

When they moved to a base on Italy's Adriatic coast, 332nd pilots were supplied with the faster, better armed P-47 Thunderbolts. These planes enabled the pilots to provide good protection for bombers.

Eaker needed fighter
pilots willing to pro-
vide close protection
to the bombers, even
if it meant not scor-
ing personal victories.
Davis knew a great
opportunity when he
saw one. His pilots
would be flying in the
offensive part of the
war, supporting the

attack on the enemy in its own terri-tory—taking the
war to the enemy, making history. "Needless to say, I
leaped at the opportunity," he said. Davis and Eaker
agreed that the 332nd would be equipped with P-47
Thunderbolts, which could fly as high and fast as the
German fighters.

As he described their new bomber escort role to his
pilots, Davis found that close support of bombers, so
unpopular with white fighter pilots, was equally unpop-

Captain Charles McGee
and his crew chief,
Sergeant Nathaniel
Wilson, at Ramitelli,
Italy in front of "Kitten."

ular with black pilots. They too wanted to be free to
break away and chase down fighters whenever they
could. Davis took a firm stand. He assembled his pilots
and described the importance of close support. He also
promised grounding and court-martial to any pilot who
left the bombers unprotected.

Late in May 1944, the 332nd joined other fighter
groups in General Eaker's 15th Air Force at Ramitelli on
the Adriatic Sea, which is the body of water separating
Italy and Yugoslavia. Davis was promoted to full colonel.
His fighters would fly bomber escort and strafing missions
to the Balkan countries—Albania, Bulgaria, Rumania
(now known as Romania), Greece, and Yugoslavia—south
and east of Germany, and to Germany, France, Spain,
Greece, and northern Italy. The strategy was to destroy
the aircraft factories, then with reduced interference from

the air, the Allies would focus on destruction of the Axis oil refineries, which were mostly in German-occupied territory to the east and south of Germany. These refineries fueled Germany's entire war machine.

On delivery, the tails of the P-47s were painted in a checkerboard design. The ground crews got out their paint cans and quickly painted the tails red, the designation for the 332nd squadrons that would earn them the nickname the Red Tail Squadrons. The 332nd pilots began trying out their P-47s in June. The P-47 was larger, faster, and more rugged than the P-39. It was fitted with front and rear armor protection for the pilot and with bulletproof glass. The fuel tanks also were bulletproof. Extra gas tanks carried on the wings provided a good range from Italy to the target areas. The plane had eight machine guns. As they made their first flights, the pilots were delighted with the speed and altitude they could attain.

The 332nd flew its first important mission as part of the 15th Air Force on June 9, 1944, three days after D-day, the Allied invasion of western Europe through Normandy, France. The mission was to escort B-17 and B-24 bombers to destroy factories in Munich, Germany. The 332nd, led by Colonel Davis, rendezvoused with the bombers, taking care to maintain an altitude and formation that would enable them to protect both the B-17s and the B-24s, which flew at different altitudes.

As they neared Munich, Colonel Davis—alerted to enemy planes approaching the bombers from the rear—

MAJOR VANCE H. MARCHBANKS'S ITALIAN CASTLE

THE "BLUE HEAVEN" OF COL. B.O. DAVIS JR.

The winters on the Adriatic coast were bitter, forcing those at Ramitelli to reinforce their quarters against the cold. This sketch drawn by a 332nd airman shows the dwelling of flight surgeon, Major Vance Marchbanks, and that of commander, Colonel Benjamin Davis. They used small gasoline stoves in their fireplaces for heat.

ordered the 302nd squadron to "Go get 'em!" At this point, two enemy planes flew through Davis's formation. Some of the 332nd fighters turned on the invaders. In the battle that followed, five enemy planes were shot down. The bombers accomplished their mission and not a single bomber was lost. The 332nd suffered one pilot lost. On the way home, the bombers were attacked again. The 332nd fought off the aggressors, damaging one enemy plane.

On their return to the base, the Red Tails received a message from one of the bomber commanders: "Your formation flying and escort is the best we have ever seen." Colonel Davis would receive the Distinguished Flying Cross for his leadership of the mission.

During most of the rest of June, the Red Tails flew bomber escort missions to Munich, Germany; Budapest, Hungary; Bratislava, Czechoslovakia; Bucharest, Rumania (now known as Romania); and Sofia, Bulgaria. They also flew strafing missions against Axis troops in Italy and German-occupied countries to the west.

On June 25, the 332nd squadrons set out to strafe enemy infantry in the Balkans and Italy. When they found no troops, the pilots continued down the Italian coast, looking for other enemy targets. Near Trieste on the Adriatic Sea, they spotted an enemy destroyer. Five Red Tails attacked the ship, even though the planes carried no bombs to use against a steel warship bristling with guns. Captain Wendell Pruitt shot at the ship, setting it on fire. Lieutenant Gwynne Pierson scored a second hit—apparently on the store of weapons, because the ship exploded and sank like a stone. The pilots then continued along the Adriatic coast, attacking radar and radio transmitters as well as truck convoys.

Back at the base, the commanding officers of the 15th Air Force were incredulous. Two fighters sank a destroyer with bullets? It was unheard of, impossible! But the fighters' wing cameras provided the proof of this incredible feat. Pruitt and Pierson earned the Distinguished Flying Cross for their achievement.

Late in June, the 332nd was supplied with new planes—P-51 Mustangs. Equipped with larger gas tanks than the P-47, the P-51 could travel farther and operate better at the high altitudes flown by the B-17 bombers.

Lieutenant C. D. "Lucky" Lester earned the right to paint three swastikas on his P-51 after he shot down three German Messerschmitts in four minutes.

The ground crews quickly painted the tails of the new planes red.

On July 3 the 99th joined the 332nd Fighter Group, making it the only fighter group to contain four squadrons. Nobody was pleased with the move. The 99th pilots felt that being detached from a white fighter group and attached to the only black one was a return to segregation. The 99th regarded the 332nd as amateurs while the 332nd feared that the 99th pilots would get all the important assignments. It took three months for Colonel Davis to iron out all the problems. But finally a team spirit developed among the squadrons.

Actually, the 99th pilots had problems of their own. For one thing, they had been flying P-40s for more than a year. Now they had to get used to the faster, more maneuverable P-51s. Two 99th pilots were killed during practice flights. Secondly, the 99th had had no squadron medical officer for many months. It is the responsibility of the medical officer to monitor the health of the people in his unit, watching in particular for signs of battle fatigue in pilots. Many members of the 99th squadron were now in poor physical condition. Some were suffering from exhaustion and battle fatigue. The segregated training system could not supply sufficient replacement pilots, so many of the 99th pilots got no rest between missions. Captain Vance Marchbanks, the 332nd flight surgeon, found it necessary to ground most of the 99th pilots for rest and treatment. All but one returned to combat after about a week.

During July, the 332nd flew many bomber escort missions to oil refineries, weapons and tank factories, and airfields. On July 12, three Red Tail squadrons flew a bomber escort mission to railroad yards in France. As they crossed the French coast, the pilots sighted 25 enemy fighters moving in to attack bombers. When the enemy planes saw the fighters, they turned away, exposing

The 332nd's major assignment was protecting bombers during their missions to destroy German factories and supply centers. This is a bomber's-eye view of the Ploesti oil fields in Rumania just as a bomb sets an oil storage tank ablaze.

themselves to attack. A group of Red Tails attacked the fleeing planes. Captain Joseph Elsberry shot down three enemy planes that crossed in front of him, one right after the other. Lieutenant Harold Sawyer destroyed the tail section of another and saw the plane crash to the earth.

By the end of July, the 332nd had scored 39 aerial victories—they had shot down 39 enemy fighters. The 332nd had also made its contribution to the Allied goal of destroying German oil refineries. The Red Tails flew bomber escort missions to the major Nazi Ploesti oil complex in Rumania (now known as Romania) and to others near Vienna. At the end of July, nearly all enemy oil refineries had been attacked by Allied planes. Officials estimated that the Allied attacks had resulted in the loss of 400 million gallons of fuel, which the enemy badly needed to power planes, tanks, and other vehicles. Enemy planes sat on runways. Tanks and trucks were frozen in their tracks. But the enemy was repairing the damage, so the Allied planes kept up the attack through the summer and fall.

In a preflight meeting, 332nd pilots are briefed on the goal of the mission, the terrain, the weather, and enemy opposition expected.

In August, the 332nd continued its bomber escort missions to enemy oil fields. The Alliods were about to begin a new offensive in southern France, and planned to invade the region on August 15. Now that war had

moved north, the Allieds needed southern French ports as entry points for troops and supplies. Assisting in the effort to reduce resistance to the Allied invaders, the 332nd escorted bombers sent to attack submarine docks, bridges, airfields, and radar stations. Once the invasion force had landed, the 332nd escorted bomber missions to attack enemy troops, bridges, and supply and communication centers.

The Allied offensive against oil refineries and airplane factories appeared to be taking its toll. By the end of August, the 332nd encountered few enemy planes. Now the Red Tails, after escorting bombers to safety, turned to attacking planes parked in airfields in German-occupied countries. In Czechoslovakia, 332nd planes

Ground crewmen check a P-51 gun and insert a rack of bullets

attacked two airfields, destroying 22 planes and damaging 83. At another airfield in Rumania (now known as Romania), the pilots spotted 150 planes, poorly camouflaged with hay; 83 of the planes were destroyed. In Yugoslavia, 36 more enemy planes parked on the ground were destroyed.

By September, the pilots of the 332nd had become known as skilled bomber escorts. Praise for the Red Tails came in from many bomber squadrons. The bomber crews felt safe when they had looked out their cockpit windows and saw the Red Tails there. On September 10, the top brass came to pay its respects—Generals Eaker, Nathan Twining, Dean Strother, and Benjamin O. Davis, Sr., Colonel Davis's father. In a full dress ceremony with the 15th Air Force band and troops passing in review, four pilots were presented with the Distinguished Flying Cross. General Davis pinned the

Brigadier General Benjamin Davis, Sr. (left) congratulates his son, Colonel Benjamin Davis, Jr. (right) on his successful completion of his European tour of duty.

medal on his son, honored for his leadership of one of the first bomber escort missions to Munich, during which five enemy planes were shot down. Captain Elsberry and Lieutenant Clarence Lester were honored for shooting down three planes each during single missions. Lieutenant Jack Holsclaw was cited for achieving two aerial victories during one mission.

Also in September came news that the Germans were manufacturing a new kind of plane, powered by a jet engine. The jet could fly much faster than a propeller-driven plane and could fly practically straight up. The Allies considered the jet a great threat to Allied fighters and hence to bombing missions. Air Force commanders called for renewed efforts to bomb enemy aircraft factories.

Despite their efforts, the Allies did not stop German production of jets. The Germans continued to manufacture the planes in camouflaged locations in caves and forests. Enemy jets began to be spotted by the the 15th Air Force fighters. The Red Tails saw two jets on December 9 during a bomber escort mission. The jets were indeed fast and could appear suddenly. But the jets made one short pass at the 332nd planes and then zoomed away. The Allied pilots realized that the German pilots were poorly trained, probably because of a shortage of fuel for training. By the end of 1944, the Red Tails had shot down 62 enemy planes and participated in the destruction of innumerable enemy targets on the ground.

During most of January 1945, the 332nd was "weathered in" by rain and snow. The squadrons flew 11 bomber escort missions to oil refineries and other targets. The weather improved in February, enabling the pilots to fly 39 missions. As they viewed mile after mile of smoking ruins and rubble from the air, the Red Tail pilots could see that the German war machine was close to total destruction. But they kept up the pressure on what was left, flying bomber escort missions to Germany, to German-occupied Hungary, Poland, Austria, and Yugoslavia. No target was insignificant.

By now, the enemy was so devastated that the Red Tails could sometimes fly low-altitude strafing missions to major German cities. In the Munich area, they destroyed bombers on the ground, locomotives, and boxcars. Occasionally, a lone enemy fighter would appear to defend its wrecked homeland, and the Red Tails would make short work of it. But the enemy was still fighting back. The 332nd lost five pilots and planes during February.

The Air Force continued to heap praise and medals on the men of the 332nd. Generals and colonels would visit, pin medals on the brave and the quick, and leave with a thumbs-up "Well done!"

In early March, Colonel Davis got a surprising and disappointing communication from headquarters. The 302nd Squadron was to be inactivated and disbanded. Though he was not told why, Davis believed that the Air Force was having trouble supplying black pilots to the four black fighter squadrons. The Air Force's segregation policy meant that black pilots could be trained only at

Tuskegee. That crowded field could not possibly do the job of supplying pilots to four fighter squadrons and the new black bomber group in training. As a result, the replacement pilot quotas of four per month per squadron were seldom met for the 332nd. While fighter pilots were supposed to rotate home to rest after 50 missions, most 332nd pilots flew more than 70 or 80 missions—and some flew more than 100 before being relieved. The 302nd squadron was inactivated with much ceremony and regret. The 302nd pilots not eligible for rotation were reassigned to the three remaining squadrons.

Later that same month, on March 24, a flight of 50 Red Tails escorted bombers on a mission to bomb a tank factory in Berlin; the 1,600-mile round trip mission was the longest ever made by fighters of the 15th Air Force. The long flight meant that the fighters had to be equipped with extra 110-gallon fuel tanks. These were not available on the base and were ordered from another base. The supply officer learned that the train delivering the fuel tanks was moving very slowly. Realizing that the tanks would not arrive in time, he sent a ground crew to meet the train. The crew, led by Sergeant George Watson, traveled all night in a truck convoy alongside the railroad tracks, met the train, stopped it, removed the tanks from the train, and transported them back to the base. By 5 A.M. on the morning of the flight, the crew was back at the base installing the fuel tanks on the planes.

As the Red Tails arrived over Berlin, they were stunned by the destruction below. A few battered anti-

An external fuel tank is installed on the underside of a P-51 wing. Such extra fuel supplies made the historic 332nd's long-distance bomber escort flight to Berlin possible.

aircraft towers struggled to defend what was left of the once-beautiful city. Though covered with wreckage and rubble, the tank factory continued to turn out Panzer tanks, so the bombers destroyed the factory.

As they left the target area, the Red Tails encountered 25 of the feared German jet fighters. When the jets attacked the bombers, a group of Red Tails went after them. The P-51 pilots, noting the poor turning capability of the jets, used the speed of the jets against them. The Red Tail pilots turned their planes swiftly from side to side as the jets pursued them causing the jets to speed ahead of the Allied guns. Then the Red Tails had the jets in front of their guns and they fired. The P-51 pilots shot down three jets and damaged several more. Three Red Tails lost their lives. The mission earned the Distinguished Unit Citation for the 332nd. The citation saluted "the conspicuous gallantry, professional skill, and determination of the pilots, together with the outstanding technical skill and devotion to duty of ground personnel."

As April ended, there were few enemy targets left. The German war machine—its troops, its factories, its supplies, its air force—was shattered. The Germans surrendered on May 6, 1945.

In mid-May it was time for more medals. Again the Generals and colonels came to the base and during several ceremonies awarded Distinguished Flying Crosses, Air Medals, Bronze Stars, and Silver Stars to members of the 332nd. During dinner with generals and colonels, Colonel Davis was told that the 332nd had achieved the distinction of never losing a bomber to an enemy fighter.

There was one more mission for the 332nd. In a 15th Air Force review over Italy, the group demonstrated all of its combat techniques to the generals and colonels watching below.

By July, the 332nd was on its way home. From June 1943, when the 99th went into combat, until May 1945 when the war in Europe ended, black pilots had built an admirable record. The 450 pilots, flying more than 1,500 missions, had destroyed 111 planes in the air, 150 planes on the ground, 1 destroyer, 57 locomotives, and numerous other enemy targets. They had been awarded 150 Distinguished Flying Crosses. Sixty-six pilots had died in battle, giving their lives for freedom for the people of Europe, a freedom they had not always enjoyed in their own country.

In 1945 in Ramitelli, Italy, Sergeant George Watson and the other members of the 366th Service Squadron stand outside their work tent. Watson is fifth from the right in the back row.

The Ground Crew: Diary From Somewhere In Italy

Sergeant George Watson served with the 366th Air Service Squadron of the 96th Service Group. Watson's unit included the mechanics, metal workers, truck drivers, cooks, carpenters, welders, and other specialists needed to keep the 332nd squadrons flying. What follows are excerpts from a diary Watson kept while serving in Italy. The first entry describes the group's arrival at its first base, in the Naples area near Capodichino, Italy.

February 28, 1944: We erected thirty tents for enlisted men and three tents for officers quarters, one kitchen tent and dispensary tent.

March 7, 1944: Aero Repair changed left flaps on P-39. Electrical shop wired more tents. Welding shop completed work on one gas tank, and welded motorcycle fender. Sheet Metal group patched a damaged right wing on P-39.

March 8, 1944: Our PX officer made a big hit with the men when he announced that rations were to be issued. We got our usual caramels and chocolates. The best of all was the issue of Coca-Colas.

March 13, 1944: The Aero Repair Section changed strut on a P-39. Removed the wings from two P-39s for repair. The Electric Shop repaired damaged wire in Engineering Section and repaired a portable generator. The welders straightened two truck bumpers. The Sheet Metal shop repaired hole in right front door of a P-39. The Propeller Department removed guns from a P-39 aircraft for repair.

March 17, 1944: We tasted enemy fire for the first time. An enemy bombardment began at 2:30 in the morning and lasted until 3:00. Men dove for their foxholes, luckily there were no casualties. I was on guard duty on the flight line. Shortly after the bombing started, I could see the German plane trying to evade the massive search lights that were crisscrossing the sky. While gazing into the sky I saw this German plane release some parachutes. Bombs floated to the earth and just before reaching the ground they went off. They destroyed a number of planes which were parked next to each other because the field was overcrowded. I ran into the tent that housed our tools and clothing and all I could hear was shrapnel cutting through the footlockers . . .

March 18, 1944: The aerial bombardment . . . fired the men with the ambition to dig and dig deep. We went to work honestly and faithfully. We realized that the impression the Jerries [Germans] left on the "Good Earth" meant that he wasn't kidding. By nightfall, every tent had a foxhole.

March 24, 1944: Motor Pool area of squadron covered with lava from [the eruption of] Mount Vesuvius.

March 26, 1944: Church services for a large number of men. Regular routine of duties. Parachute Section inspected five parachutes. Paint shop prepared signs. Armament crew cleaned machine guns [on planes].

April 1, 1944: The Armament Shop dismantled and cleaned left wing gun on P-39, installed right wing gun, and replaced fuselage ammunition boxes. The Prop section removed and installed new propeller on a P-39 . . . a damaged wing tip, belly cowl, air scoop, and fuselage on a P-39 were repaired. Aero Section . . . picked up a wrecked airplane.

April 2, 1944: Spring has come to the Capodichino Airfield and more than ever comes the longing for home. We know we have a job to finish, so only memories of home give us that will to "do or die" and hope for a hasty and peaceful end to the great world conflict.

April 3, 1944: . . . The Parachute Section installed a sewing machine and repaired flying clothing. . . .

April 4, 1994: . . . the Instrument Shop installed Pitot-static tube and directional compass, and checked altimeter air speed indicator and rate-of-climb indicator.

April 15, 1944: Regular routine duties on the line and in the area after a hectic early rising. At approximately 3:00 A.M. there was an air raid . . . lasting for about twenty minutes. Once again we had to hit our foxholes . . . No bombs were dropped over the immediate area or on the field, therefore there were no casualties. The next morning found the men digging deeper. . . .

April 18, 1944: Electrical section checked [plane's] electrical system, installed and timed magnetos, installed spark plug tips and batteries. Armament Crew cleaned cannon of P-39 and repacked eight chutes, and repaired flying clothing and flying goggles.

April 24, 1944: . . . The night was marred by another visit from Jerry. There were no casualties, but we hugged our foxholes and sent a prayer upward.

June 4, 1944: . . . Trips, long and tiresome, were made over mountains to depots in far distant towns for parts and supplies. Never ending, always tiresome, but never grumbling on the part of the men. That's the spirit that the 366th was born with. . . .

August 7, 1944: . . . In the evening a gigantic Red Cross show was held in the 332nd area, and transportation was furnished to the members of the squadron to witness it. Coffee and doughnuts were served by a beauty from the other side of the water. A good time was had by all. . . .

A 302nd Fighter Pilot in Combat Over Europe

Lieutenant Vernon Haywood's squadron arrived in Italy in January 1944. These are some of his memories of combat.

"We were based at Capodichino Field, just south of Naples. Our assignment was to protect the harbor from German planes. The Germans had this plane that could do everything—the ZU-88. It could fly close to the water—about 50 feet. Then it could zoom up high to maybe 30,000 feet. It was fast. It could carry bombs and a lot of fuel. These ZU-88s would come in during the day time to take photos of our ships in the harbor below. Then when the German bombers came in at night, they had the photos and they knew just where to drop their bombs.

"We'd get up high and watch for these planes. They were hard to see because they were camouflaged and looked just like the surface of the ocean. But British radar would alert us to them just below us. We never chased after them. As soon as they spotted us, they headed out to sea. They knew we carried only a small amount of fuel and couldn't chase them. We never got one of those ZU-88's. But at least we scared them away from their photo mission."

Haywood's most frightening moment in combat came during his time at Capodichino, a base crowded with British and American planes.

"Our squadron patrolled the harbor during the day, from one hour before sunrise to one hour after sunset. At night, British planes called Bullfighters, took over harbor patrol. This meant that at night there was no traffic in or out of the field. At night,

the area surrounding the base became a free-fire zone—any plane that approached would be fired on, no questions asked—by British antiaircraft gun crews who guarded the field.

"One late afternoon as we were preparing to return to base on schedule, we were asked to stay

Lieutenant Vernon Haywood in the cockpit of his fighter plane.

a little longer until the British could get there. Finally the British arrived and we headed for home. It was night and we called the base tower to tell them we were coming in.

"But as we neared the base and started spacing out for landing, all hell broke loose. The sky just lit up; there were tracer bullets everywhere.

"I was leading the flight of four planes. We were about 1,500 feet off the ground and had our landing gears down. I pulled up my wheels, moved down to 500 feet where the bullets couldn't get me and got out of there. Everybody else followed. I didn't stop to ask any questions, I just moved out of the area.

"Then after I got a safe distance away, I called the tower again and told them who we were. The firing quit and we came back in and landed. It turned out there was some kind of communication foul-up between the tower and the British. The next day, the British air marshall came over and apologized."

After a few months, Haywood's squadron moved from Capodichino to Ramitelli in eastern Italy. Eventually they were provided with P-51 fighters, which could fly faster and farther.

"After we got our new planes, Colonel Davis told us that we had to fly close escort to the bombers. We didn't like that idea much. We were pretty eager— wanted to be Aces and get our names in the paper.

"But Davis told us we couldn't leave those bombers and go off chasing fighters the way those white guys did. Davis said that even if we shot down 10 fighters, all we had to do was lose one bomber—that's 12 guys inside—to a fighter and the Army would be ready to bring the whole outfit home. There were so many people back home who didn't think we should be there in the first place. We just couldn't afford it, he told us. That's why we stuck close to those bombers. Back home they were saying we couldn't do it." *No enemy fighter ever downed a bomber guarded by Tuskegee Airmen.*

In his P-51, Haywood led fighters on bomber escort missions that struck at German supplies. They strafed oil barges on the Danube River and trains and trucks carrying fuel. They escorted bombers to destroy oil refineries in Poland.

"Fire was our clue that a bomber had scored a hit on a refinery or oil field. But Intelligence figured out that the Germans were starting fires to make us think we had hit the target. Orders went out to blanket oil fields with bombs."

Haywood will never forget some of his bomber escort missions. Bombers must take a fixed path or course, called an RP, once they near the target. They can't veer from that course because the bombardier needs a course he can count on so that his bomb drop will hit the target.

"The Germans had hundreds of these 88-millimeter antiaircraft guns. Very accurate. They would just aim these guns straight up and send up a blanket of fire when they detected the bombers.

"When the bombers started on their RP, we pulled away to the other side of the target. But these bombers had to fly straight into this black cloud of German antiaircraft fire because they were on their bomb run, RP. They had to take their chances with the flak and hope they hit their target.

"I had an awful lot of respect for those bomber pilots. We fighter pilots could actually see the flak from the other side. I knew what the bomber crews must be seeing. We couldn't help them in there. All we could do was fight off the enemy fighters who certainly wouldn't go into that cloud of flak to attack them.

"We would meet the bombers on the other side of the target, protect them from the enemy fighters who were waiting there, and escort them safely out of enemy territory.

"Some of the bombers came out smoking, missing a wing or part of an engine. I remember looking into the flak and seeing one bomber just disintegrate—just small pieces floating down. No parachutes. They must have taken a hit directly into the bomb bay door.

One combat mission Haywood will never forget had a very surprising result. The four squadrons of the 332nd were assigned to strafe a crowded airfield in Rumania. There were about 250 enemy planes— fighters, bombers, gliders—parked wing to wing on the field.

One 332nd squadron moved in first to attack the guns defending the field. They reported no return fire. No one shot back! Haywood was in one of the squadrons assigned to attack the planes.

"It was a picture-perfect target—this grassy field, jam-packed with planes all lined up. We had practiced this in the States. Keep your eye on the target. Keep your wings straight. Go in. But we never dreamed we'd ever see anything like this in combat—with nobody shooting at us.

"We set up our gunnery patterns, making strafing runs just like we did in training. We could see our bullets hitting the planes. Pieces of the planes were flying in the air. But the planes weren't exploding. I remember one plane in particular. I flew down really low and shot up under the wing at the gas tank. Nothing. It didn't explode.

"Suddenly, it dawned on us. The planes were out of fuel. That's why they didn't explode. Back at the base, other pilots had similar reports. All of those attacks on oil fields, oil barges, and synthetic oil refineries had taken their toll on the German's supply of aviation fuel. That was why we hadn't been seeing many German planes in the air recently."

It was September 1944. By the spring of the next year, the Germans would surrender.

Chapter Six

THE 477TH
BOMBARDMENT GROUP

It was January 1944. The 99th Fighter Squadron achieved major victories in aerial combat over Italy. The 332nd Fighter Group had arrived in Italy to undertake what was to become a triumphant and highly honored combat record. And, the 477th Bombardment Group was activated. This bomber group was destined never to battle in foreign lands, freeing citizens of other countries from fascism. Theirs would be a battle against racism, what some termed the American brand of fascism. During this struggle, one black officer declared that "racial bias is fascistic, un-American and directly contrary to the ideas for which I am willing to fight and die."

Lieutenant General Ira Eaker (at the microphone) speaks at the ceremonies activating the 477th Bombardment Group. Behind him are Brigadier General Benjamin Davis, Sr. and War Department civilian aide, Truman Gibson.

Like the 99th, the 477th was established because of pressure from black ministers and other black leaders. The leaders realized that the experience gained flying a bomber, a large multiengine plane similar to a passenger plane, would be valuable flying experience in the postwar world. It would be bomber pilots, not fighter pilots, who would be the airline pilots of the future. Additional pressure from the War Department resulted in the Air Force issuing a plan for the activation of a black bombardment group, the 477th Bombardment Group.

The Air Force had only a half-hearted interest in the project. Within the Air Force plan itself were the words, "It is common knowledge that the colored race does not have the technical nor the flying background for the creation of a bombardment-type unit."

A World War II bomber crew included 12 men with many talents—pilots, navigators, bombardiers, and gunners. A bombardment group also needed ground crews to service the bombers. The Air Force proposed that pilots learn to fly twin-engine planes at Tuskegee and to pilot B-25 bombers at Mather Field, California. Ground crews would learn aircraft servicing at Mather, moving on to Inglewood, California where bomber manufacturers would provide additional training. Gunners would train at Eglin Field, Florida, while navigator-bombardiers would train at fields in New Mexico and Texas. The home

Pilots preparing to join the 477th Bombardment Group practice twin-engine flying over Tuskegee Army Air Field.

base of the 477th would be Selfridge Field, near Detroit. After learning their individual jobs, the men would begin training there as a bomber crew. Training for the various crew members usually began at least six months before the activation of a new bombardment group. But the 477th was activated without trained manpower.

Colonel Robert Selway, Jr., a white West Point graduate, was appointed commander of the group. He began bringing in his staff at Selfridge in mid-January 1944. White supervisory officers were brought in from combat and from stateside bases. Sixty black pilots reported, but everyone else needed to man the group was still in training or had not even begun training.

The most important part of bomber training was training as a crew. But this was not pos-

Wearing his cold weather gear, a 617th Bomber Squadron crewman mans the defensive machine gun (waist gun) in the middle of the bomber.

sible for the 477th in early 1944 because individual crew members had yet to complete their technical training. For months, pilots monotonously went through their exercises without navigator-bombardiers or gunners. A year later, the 477th was still not fully manned, lacking 70 pilots, two navigator-bombardiers, and all 288 gunners. Not until March 1945 was the group fully manned. As men arrived, the three squadrons that would make up the 477th Group—the 617th, 618th, and 619th—were formed.

While personnel problems obstructed bomber crew training, the 477th faced even bigger problems with its commanding officer, Colonel Selway, and the racist atmosphere at Selfridge. Selway was among those in the Air Force who thought blacks lacked the skill, attitude, and intelligence to be combat pilots. He would not permit blacks to be supervisors of squadrons, ground crews, or of any other activity on the base. He was insensitive to the needs of his men and did not take the time to put himself in their place to understand the pressures they felt. Selway was anxious to toe the Air Force line when it came to segregation, as the Air Force sought to find ways to ignore certain War Department orders.

Selfridge Field had been the scene of racial unrest before the 477th arrived. The problems stemmed from the attitude of Major General Frank Hunter, commander of the First Air Force. Hunter believed that "racial friction will occur if colored and white pilots are teamed together." In the previous year, black officers had used the officers club at Selfridge. (The officers club was a major source of entertainment for officers and their families, offering bars, restaurants, game rooms, and other diversions.) In late 1943, Hunter issued orders that blacks could not use the club and would have to wait until one was built for them. Hunter's order was in conflict with

Army Regulation 210-10 (AR 210-10), which specifically stated that all officers on a post could be members of officers clubs, messes, and similar social organizations at that post.

Black officers arriving at Selfridge to join the 477th attempted to enter the officers club and were refused admission. Hunter heard about the black officers' violation of his orders and went into action. On a rainy Thursday in March, loudspeakers called the officers to a meeting in the base theater. Radio messages ordered pilots to return to the base for the meeting. In the base theater, "Tenshun" called the officers to attention. Hunter marched down the aisle and laid it on the line, saying that the War Department was not ready to recognize blacks as the social equals of whites and that it was not the time for blacks to fight for equal rights. Hunter said blacks should prove themselves in combat first. "This is my airfield. As long as I am commander of the First Air Force, there will be no racial mixing at any post under my command. Anyone who protests will be sought out and dealt with."

Hunter left, but his orders affected all blacks on the base. Racial discrimination intensified. Black families were denied base housing. Blacks were not promoted. When a white commanding officer was transferred, another white was brought in to take his place. The black officers were the assistants; many white supervisors did little work and got the promotions.

The black officers wrote letters of protest to the President, to reporters, and to the National Association for the Advancement of Colored People (NAACP). The letters and protests produced results. The War Department, pressured by congressmen and black leaders, sent an Air Force inspector to Selfridge to study the situation and make recommendations. The inspector reported that the main problems were "outside agitation and communists from Detroit." He also identified the black press as trying to stir up racial unrest. The best thing to do, he advised, was to move the 477th away from Detroit.

In early May, 1944 the members of the 477th were told to send their families home. The men were told they were moving to a secret location. Early one morning the troops, in full dress uniform, were loaded onto a train. With shades drawn, the train headed north from Detroit into Canada, then east and south back into the United States at Buffalo, New York; from there the train went to Gary, Indiana, and on to its final destination— Louisville, Kentucky. The men were told to get off the train. They had no idea where they were. Facing them were armed troops in full battle dress lined up along the platform. Greatly alarmed, someone asked what was going on and where they were. There was no answer. Then after 15 minutes the troops left. Their commander had been told some "bad niggers" were coming in and this was his way of meeting their train.

The 477th's new base was Godman Field, Kentucky, near Fort Knox. The official reason given for moving the group was the bad weather and industrial smoke in the Detroit area. But the 477th knew better. There at

Godman, they were isolated from the press and from black leaders. They had been moved to the South, where people "knew how to handle blacks." Nearby at Fort Knox, large police and tank battalions were available to deal with any black rebellion.

Godman Field was inadequate for training a bomber group. Its runways were too short and too damaged to handle bombers. There was too little hangar or parking space for the bombers. The area was unsuitable for night flying, and there was no target area for gunnery practice. Flying visibility was obscured by smoke and tank dust from Fort Knox. Colonel Selway vowed to fix the deficiencies. Hangars and runways were repaired and enlarged. Bases in Indiana and South Carolina were selected for night flying and gunnery practice. The result was a complicated, unwieldy training schedule that forced the men to commute from base to base so that they could train.

Recreational facilities were no better than the training facilities. Nearby towns welcomed blacks to few of their facilities. Blacks could use any facility at the field, but there wasn't much from which to choose. One building served as gym, theater, dance hall, and schoolroom. The 477th black officers were housed in barracks built for enlisted men, and had full use of an officers club not much bigger than a large office. The white 477th officers stayed at Fort Knox and used the officers club there.

The black officers decided to use the Fort Knox officers club. They tried to enter the club and were refused.

The Fort Knox commander complained to Colonel Selway, telling Selway to keep his black troops away. After all "his boys," black Fort Knox Army officers, knew better. Selway's black flyers could ruin the good manners of the Fort Knox "boys."

Morale among blacks of the 477th began to fall. Training was not going well. Of the 128 navigator-bombardiers needed, only 23 had arrived by October, 1945. Later that fall, more pilots and bombardiers arrived, but the bombardiers had not had their navigation training. Finally, at year's end there were enough people to begin training a few bomber crews. But then winter, with clouds that reduced visibility and freezing temperatures that produced wing icing, sharply reduced flying time.

A group of black officers wrote to Eleanor Roosevelt, the first lady, describing their unit's problems and pointing

Navigators train before reporting to their 477th squadrons.

out that they deserved the same rights as white officers. To avoid the camp censor, who would have given the letter to Selway, the black officers drove to Louisville and mailed it there. Several days later, a wire from the War Department, written at the direction of the President and inquiring about the officers' grievances, arrived on Selway's desk. A day later, Lieutenant General Barney Giles from Air Force headquarters came to Godman to investigate. Although the black officers said little in the meetings because Selway was present, the general was very perceptive.

General Giles issued a report to the War Department and the President that accurately reflected the problems of the black officers. Morale was low because of racism and because Selway didn't even acknowledge its existence. (He was fond of saying to anyone who asked, "There is no racial problem here and there will be no racial problem here.") Black officers were not promoted to responsible positions and resented being stationed in the South, which was unfriendly to blacks. In summary, Giles reported that the 477th's problem was Selway and his attitude. The Air Force took no action.

In early 1945, the Air Force decided that Godman Field was too small for the 477th and made plans to move the group to Freeman Field in Indiana. The large, well-equipped base would make it possible to combine the many aspects of bomber training in one place, and would be an ideal place in which to ready the 477th for combat.

But Selway did not have training on his mind as he made his plans for the move. He thought he had finally found a way to fulfill the Air Force's wish for segregation in officers clubs. Selway wanted to get ahead in the Air Force, to make general perhaps, and he intended to do his best to please the Air Force higher-ups. What he needed was a legal way to segregate, and he thought he had found it. Another Army regulation (AR 210-6) said that a base commander could designate the use of officers clubs according to units or assignments. Using this regulation, Selway could segregate without ever mentioning race, something very important to Major General Hunter. It was beautiful, he thought.

The 477th began its move to Freeman Field on March 1, 1945. Among the other Selway directives about the new base was one that designated Club One for officer trainees and Club Two for key supervisory and instructor officers. Officers were assigned by name to each club. Several black officers, among them the flight surgeon and the chaplain, were certainly not trainees and yet they were assigned to Club One, the trainee club. The order's intent was clear to everyone.

Black officers immediately named Club One "Uncle Tom's Cabin" to show they knew segregation when they saw it. In an effort to desegregate Club One, black officers elected their white squadron leader to the club board. Groups of black officers began to wander into the supervisory Club Two and request service. When they were denied service, some black officers left; others stayed, sitting at tables or playing the slot machines. Selway was sick with the flu at the time. When he recovered, he called the black officers together and ordered them to use Club One.

Selway decided to write a detailed order defining the use of every building on the base. The first page of the new order, to be effective April 1945, listed the goals of the new order: development of individual and unit combat spirit and conservation of energy. A five-page table followed, listing each building and its use. Club One was designated for officer trainees, Club Two for supervisory and instructor officers. The flight surgeon and the chaplain were reclassified so that they fit into designation for trainees.

The order was posted on April 1, and blacks stayed away from Club Two. The new order seemed to be working. Selway was delighted. What he didn't know then was that the black officers had a plan. The plan called for nonviolent action that would highlight the Air Force segregation policy and the failure of the Air Force to implement AR 210-10. In groups, the black officers would peacefully try to enter Club Two. There would be no angry words or fighting. If they were arrested, they would go quietly with the military police. The idea was to get all the officers arrested if necessary. Then they would get word of their plight to black and white newspapers, the NAACP, and other groups.

The black officers' plan went into effect on April 5, the day a large group of trainees flew in from Godman.

Selway had learned of the plan and had posted a provost marshall at the door of Club Two. Four black officers began the Club Two campaign at 9:15 that evening and were arrested. Thirty minutes later, nineteen more followed. Then three more, who shoved their way past the provost marshall, entered. All were arrested. Fourteen more black officers followed, then more until the club closed for the night. A total of 69 black officers, who claimed that AR 210-10 gave them the right to use Club Two, were arrested for trying to exercise that right. In the next two days, more black officers were arrested.

Air Force lawyers studied Selway's April 1 order and called it unclear. It was quite obvious to them that the intent was to designate one officers club for whites and one for blacks. On April 7, the Air Force ordered the release of all the black officers, except for the three who forced their way into the club.

Selway closed Club Two and, with Major General Hunter's help, wrote a new order. But the new regulation still did not deal logically with the membership of the black flight surgeon, the chaplain, and a few other non-trainee officers. Attached to the order was a statement that each officer was required to sign. The statement said that the signer had read and understood the order. All the white officers and most of the black officers signed the statement. But 101 black officer trainees refused to sign. A day later, despite a direct order from Selway and from their squadron leader, the 101 still refused to sign. (It is a serious offense in time of war to refuse the order of a superior officer.) The 101 officers were arrested and flown to Godman, where they were placed in barracks guarded by armed Fort Knox troops. Despite the fact that their barracks were guarded, the 101 imprisoned black officers managed to get word out about what had happened to them by dropping letters and news releases into convertibles driven close to the barracks windows by wives and friends.

By mid-April the NAACP was protesting the arrest of the 101 to the President. The Urban League asked for Congress to investigate the racist promotion practices of the 477th commanders. A number of important senators began pressing the War Department about the matter.

By April 20, the pressure put on the Air Force had its effect. On that day, Army Chief of Staff George Marshall ordered that all 101 black officers be released and that all charges against them be dropped. Marshall also ordered that the three officers charged with using force to enter Club Two be court-martialed. (Later, all three officers were found not guilty of the most serious charge against them, but one was convicted of offering violence against a superior officer and fined $150.)

On April 26, in the midst of all the congressional and public protest of events at Freeman, the Air Force shipped the 477th back to Godman Field. It had become clear that Godman was a place where troops were sent to be punished. The constantly interrupted training, the poor facilities at Godman, and the racist policies finally took their toll. The 477th practically collapsed as a unit. The men now realized that the Air Force was willing to sacrifice training for segregation. They lost their desire to train well and serve their country; all they wanted was to get out. They refused to salute white officers—even Colonel Selway, the base commander. In five air accidents over the next few months, eleven men were killed.

The War Department's McCloy Committee, which had investigated the alleged bad combat record of the 99th, now launched an investigation of the Freeman Field events. Its final report, issued on May 18, 1945, labeled Selway's actions "not in accord with existing regulations." Early in June, an officer from the Pentagon arrived at Godman to relieve Selway of his command. Replacing him would be Colonel Benjamin Davis, Jr., commander of the 332nd Fighter Group, soon to return from Europe, where the war had ended.

On July 1, 1945, in a ceremony marked by marching troops and speeches, there was a change of command.

Colonel Robert Selway, commander of the 477th Bombardment Group.

Lieutenant General Ira Eaker, the Air Force's acting chief of staff, began by praising Colonel Davis's combat record. Then Eaker had important news for the group. The 477th would become a composite group, with two bomber squadrons and one fighter squadron. The 477th would, Eaker promised, be in combat in the Pacific Theater by the coming October. Davis would select his own staff and supervise the final preparations and combat training. At a ceremony in the base theater, later that day, Eaker relieved Selway and his staff of their duties. He then looked at the assembled men of the 477th, gestured toward Colonel Davis, and formally introduced the new commander of Godman Field.

Morale rose at Godman. Colonel Davis began the task of getting the 477th ready for combat. But the 477th would never see combat. Everyone had expected a long, costly war against the Japanese in the Pacific. But two atomic bombs dropped by the American bombers on the Japanese cities of Hiroshima and Nagasaki changed all that. Japan surrendered in August 1945.

The men of the 477th earned no ribbons for combat. But they had fought the "battle of Godman" and the "Freeman campaign." These battles used tactics that would be put to use in the civil rights demonstrations of the 1960s, including nonviolent sit-ins. The goals such tactics were intended to achieve—equal opportunity, a just society, simple fairness—had been around for a long time.

Family Life at Godman

*T**he Allies won World War II in Europe in June 1945. All over the United States, members of the 332nd Fighter Squadron returned home to their families. Lois Marchbanks was living on the Tuskegee Institute campus when her husband, 332nd flight surgeon Major Vance Marchbanks, came home from the war. Following are Mrs. Marchbanks's memories of her husband's return.*

"We were so excited. The train coming into the station at Chehaw, near Tuskegee, was supposed to arrive at 10:30 P.M. But it was late. We waited and watched. Finally the train came in—but no Vance. I didn't know what to think. Then I heard a voice calling 'Lois! Lois!' I looked down the track and there was Vance lugging his bags from way down at the end of the train far from the station. Only white people could sit in the front of the train. He had to sit in the last car and that's where he had to get off.

"Vance had been gone for a year and a half. Four-year-old Roslyn remembered her daddy. But Vance had never seen 20-month old Joy. She stared at him and said nothing. For the next few days, she addressed all her comments to him through me. 'Mommy, tell that man. . . .'"

The 332nd was ordered to report to Godman Field, Kentucky, where the squadron would prepare to enter the war against Japan in the South Pacific. There would be quarters for families at Godman.

"That was good news. We knew it wouldn't be elaborate. But after the long separation, it would be good to see Vance on a daily basis."

Lois Marchbanks remembers Godman Field as a barren place—no grass, just this small group of gray wooden buildings. The families were to stay in two of the barracks buildings, 20 or 30 families in each two-story building.

"We just had sleeping rooms, one for the husband and wife, another for children. There were few children there. These were young men. Most had no children.

"There were two bathrooms on each floor with a couple of showers, maybe four toilet stalls and three or four sinks. One bathroom was for women and children and the other for men.

"We ate in the officers mess. That was a real nuisance because I had to put the girls in fresh clothes three times a day. But Vance usually ate with us and that was great.

Left to right: front, Roslyn and Joy Marchbanks; back row, Lois and Vance Marchbanks and Colonel Benjamin Davis.

"The girls loved it at Godman. They had a few playmates. There were sandboxes and swings for them. The weather was good. Sometimes they would show cartoons in the mess hall for the kids."

The Godman administration had done its best to meet the needs of the families. They were supplied with linen and towels, and there was a laundromat for personal laundry. Major Marchbanks ran the small clinic at the field. There, minor ailments of service people and families were treated. Serious illnesses were treated at nearby Fort Knox Hospital.

Black families could shop at the Fort Knox post exchange for items such as toothpaste and adult clothing. There was a separate movie theater for blacks. But other Fort Knox facilities such as the golf course, swimming pool, and gyms were off-limits to blacks.

As Lois Marchbanks soon found out, Fort Knox schools were also off-limits. "I remember Lucille Gleed, wife of Major Edward Gleed, took her 6-year-old daughter, Betty, to the Fort Knox school on the first day of school. It was the first week in September and time for the child to start her schooling. By the time Lucille got home from dropping Betty off, she had a phone call. She was told by school officials to come and get her daughter. Betty couldn't attend the school because she didn't live on Fort Knox. Of course, we all knew that wasn't the real reason. Lucille had to leave Godman and take her children back to Kansas where Betty could begin school."

The Marchbanks family sometimes went to Louisville for an outing. They would eat in the "colored only" restaurants and attend the "colored" theaters. Once when they were in the city, they went shopping for shoes for Roz.

"What size does she wear?" asked the shoe store clerk.

"Measure her foot," said Lois Marchbanks.

"I'll make a tracing of her foot on this paper and fit it into the shoe," said the clerk.

"You're not going to fit her with shoes using a tracing," said Lois Marchbanks.

"Well, she can't try on shoes in this store," said the clerk.

"Then we don't want any shoes," said Lois Marchbanks.

That a child could be treated this way was appalling to Lois Marchbanks. She sent away to Best and Company in New York City for the shoes.

Despite it all, the Marchbanks family enjoyed being together for the first time in a year and a half. "We made the best of it," said Lois Marchbanks. "It was the military. We took it as it came. I had a nice life in the military—nice life, nice people. I made many good friends. Wouldn't trade it for anything.

"We knew Godman was temporary. It was great to be with Vance after such a long time, especially since we believed he would soon be going overseas again. But it really upset me that Betty couldn't go to school. That was a dirty deal."

The service families at Godman Field treat themselves to a picnic. Front left: Lucille Gleed and her daughter Betty.

Japan surrendered in August 1945. And the 477th stood down from its preparation for combat. In 1946 the group moved to Lockbourne Air Force Base, near Columbus, Ohio. There the Marchbanks *family was assigned regular family living quarters. Their first assignment after integration was March Field in California, where their family quarters were very nice. Equally nice were the accommodations at Loring Air Force Base in Maine and the base in Okinawa.* "We made friends with many white families, and I still hear from some of them," said Lois Marchbanks.

Chapter Seven

BLACK AND WHITE TOGETHER

In May 1945, just after the war in Europe ended, the senior commanders of black units reported to the War Department on the record of blacks in combat. They made recommendations about the best way to use black troops in the postwar world.

Lieutenant Colonel Louis Nippert, an Army Air Force staff officer, summarized the reports: "Negro officers are below average in common sense, imagination, resourcefulness, aggressiveness, sense of responsibility, and in their ability to make decisions. They accept lower standards and make allowances for misbehavior. Enlisted men are not dependable, are careless with equipment, are not industrious, and consider discrimination a reason for their assignments. The feeling of being discriminated against is considered the greatest shortcoming of Negro soldiers." Nippert found that, for the most part, individual reports considered the cause of most black shortcomings to be "environmental"—the result of poor education and training as well as lack of technical work experience in civilian life. This was, at least, an improvement over the 1925 War College study that found that blacks had small brains and were inherently inferior to whites.

The Nippert report recommended that blacks should be recruited and trained for all Air Force specialties. However, despite the fact that some commanders believed segregation badly interfered with training and job performance, Nippert recommended that segregation should continue.

The War Department decided to probe further and study the black combat record. It created a board of four generals, headed by Lieutenant General Alvan Gillem, to design a policy for using blacks in the Air Force. The Gillem Board examined the Nippert report and interviewed many officers who contributed to it. The board also interviewed some civilian leaders who had not been consulted by Nippert. Some witnesses, such as William Hastie, the former civilian aide to the secretary of war, called for "immediate integration."

Perhaps the most eloquent argument for integration came from a white man, Tuskegee Air Field commander Colonel Noel Parrish, who accused the Air Force of dealing with the issue of race in an unconstitutional way: "Whether we dislike or like Negroes and whether they like or dislike us," he said, "under the Constitution of the United States, which we are all sworn to uphold, they are citizens of the United States, having the same rights and privileges of other citizens and entitled to the same applications and protection of the laws."

The Gillem board also heard from other high-ranking white combat officers, most of whom opposed integration. Air Force commander Carl Spaatz testified that black pilots and mechanics were such low achievers that he doubted they "could stand the pace if integrated into white crews." Air Staff Chief General Ira Eaker, the man who gave the 332nd their important bomber escort assignment, testified that blacks and whites do not do "their best work when integrated." Others testified that black officers were ineffective—they lacked leadership, initiative, aggressiveness, and dependability.

The Gillem board weighed the negative testimony of high ranking officers against that of supporters of integration, most of whom were civilians. The board also considered studies of blacks and whites. In one such study, the board saw increased white acceptance of blacks. Another study showed that blacks were becoming more skilled and better educated.

The Gillem board then issued a recommendation to the War Department calling for limited integration at first, with the long-range goal of full integration. The board also suggested the formation of War Department General Staff Groups that would deal with minority problems and help implement the board's recommendation.

The Gillem report was sent to Army commanders in the form of a pamphlet entitled, "Utilization of Negro Manpower in the Postwar Army Policy." But the general staff groups were not formed, and most commanders simply ignored the policy. They also ignored the instruction pamphlet designed to help troops understand the reason for integration.

While the discussion of integration and segregation was taking place, segregation went on for the 477th Composite Group. Called by some "Ben Davis's Air Force," a reference to its black separateness, the 477th finally managed to move away from dilapidated Godman Field to a better place. It hadn't been easy. The Air Force had considered two fields—one near Hartford,

Connecticut, and the other near Columbus, Ohio. But the leaders of both cities raised loud objections to siting a large group of blacks nearby. The Air Force, working through a few Ohio congressmen, finally quieted the furor in Columbus, and the 477th was assigned to Lockbourne Air Field, south of Columbus.

Columbus's black citizens proudly turned out to welcome the 477th. But *The Columbus Citizen,* the city's morning paper, called the 477th a bunch of troublemakers and objected to American "servants" doing America's fighting. Despite this unfriendly welcome, the 477th eagerly began refurbishing their new base, which had been largely unused since the end of the war.

Colonel Davis struggled endlessly with the personnel problems created by segregation. At first he had too many pilots. Then, shortly after the end of the war, he had too few, as many of his trained and experienced men left the service. Pilot training had been terminated at Tuskegee Air Field, and black pilots were now being trained at Randolph Field, Texas, but in insufficient numbers. Davis had too many navigator-bombardiers and not enough pilots. In some instances, training of blacks in other skills wasn't taking place at all. Because whites could not be assigned to a black commander, Davis could not request the specialists he needed from the white ranks. By the same token, the black specialists assigned to him could not be reassigned to a white unit in which they were needed.

In July 1947, the 477th Composite Group was reorganized into the 332nd Fighter Wing. Bomber pilots were trained to fly fighters. But 25 bomber crewmen were left with no assignment, even though the white bomber groups needed specialists with their skills.

Lockbourne's personnel problems stemmed in part from a memo written by Assistant Chief of Air Staff Lieutenant General Hoyt Vandenberg to Chief of the Air Force General Henry Arnold: "Due to lower average intelligence, the demonstrated lack of leadership, general poor health, and extremely high elimination rate in training, it is far more expensive to train Negro officer personnel than white . . . Due to excessive cost of training Negro air crew and commissioned personnel, as well as the generally poor results obtained from graduates, further training of Negro personnel is not economically sound." Vandenberg's memo also firmly backed segregation. Whites insist on it, he wrote, and to avoid trouble "segregation is essential."

As a result of Vandenberg's memo, many blacks were forced into unskilled Air Force assignments. With the war to defend democracy won—a war in which they had fought—many blacks back from the war were not about to accept segregation and discrimination anymore. Many were well educated. Many had learned technical skills in the Air Force and could not accept janitorial and kitchen work in the peacetime Air Force. They had traveled to other parts of the world, where they had learned how it felt to be treated the same as other people. They had supported the goals of the war—justice, equality, and freedom for people in other countries. Now they claimed those rights for black Americans.

In their frustration and anger, some black service people protested. At Fort Worth Airfield, Texas, 1,000 black airmen signed a letter to a newspaper that described their life as "unbearable, un-American, prejudiced, discriminatory, and segregative." They charged that "98 percent of the colored soldiers on this station" are used as kitchen workers, janitors, and street sweepers. They complained that the club, the recreation areas, and the post exchange were too small. A one-chair barbershop was supposed to serve 1,000 black servicemen. A few weeks later, their anger erupted into a riot over the use of the service club.

In September 1947 the Air Force became a separate service, no longer a part of the Army. Stuart Symington, who was appointed the first secretary of the new Air Force, believed in integration. So did some of the junior officers enrolled in courses at the Air Force War, staff, and command colleges, where future generals were trained. Their opinions mirrored a changing view in the new generation of Air Force command officers. Each student officer was required to write a paper. In their papers, three such officers wrote:

Segregation is the refusal to apply the American system to Negro individuals. Colonel Noel Parrish

The armed forces of the United States cannot afford to subscribe to any doctrine based on a premise of permanent racial superiority any more than they can afford to wage

war with antiquated weapons . . . It is the mission of the military to educate bigots, thereby producing a more efficient force. Lieutenant Colonel Solomon Cutcher

As a nation we have wasted energy in perpetrating the wasteful and sterile luxury of segregation . . . We have actually wasted the human resources of Negro Americans by submitting them to a relentless system of frustration and rejection. Major Hugh D. Young

The Air Force's new head of personnel, Lieutenant General Idwal Edwards, had long believed that segregation was wasteful and inefficient. Given the natural talents and aptitudes of people, he believed that it was unreasonable to expect that training could be tailored to meet the exact personnel needs of a black unit. Some blacks ended up being trained for something for which they had no aptitude or interest because that was what the black unit needed. Others worked at assignments for which they had not been trained, thereby wasting their training.

Edwards sent a report describing the inefficiencies of segregation to the new Air Force chief, General Carl Spaatz. In public statements, Spaatz as well as other Air Force officials, agreed that the Air Force must eliminate segregation.

During this time there was also antisegregation activity in the White House. In October 1947, President Harry Truman's Committee on Civil Rights issued a report entitled "To Secure These Rights." One of its recommendations for ensuring people's rights called for Congress to pass laws banning discrimination and segre-

gation in the armed forces. In February 1948, the President sent the recommendations of the report to Congress as a proposed civil rights bill. His proposal caused an uproar in Congress, especially among some Southerners, who called the bill "devastating and obnoxious."

In July 1948, after Congress had refused to act on the Civil Rights Bill, the President, as commander in chief of the armed forces, issued Executive Order 9981. This was, in effect, a military order to end segregation in the armed forces. The President also appointed a committee to make certain that desegregation took place.

The President's order was all that Air Force Secretary Symington needed. Symington issued his own order to integrate the Air Force and met with his generals to discuss the order. Despite their public statements, many of these high-ranking officers turned out to be against integration. But they did not want to say that to their boss,

In July 1948 President Harry Truman signed Executive Order 9981, calling for integation of the Armed Services. Left to right: Seated, Secretary of Defense James V. Forrestal, President Harry S Truman, Alphonsus J. Donahue; Standing, John H. Sengstacke, William E. Stevenson, Secretary of the Army Kenneth C. Royall, Secretary of the Air Force W. Stuart Symington, Lester B. Granger, Dwight R. G. Palmer, Secretary of the Navy John L. Sullivan and Truman's committee chairman Charley Fahy. Granger was executive director of the Urban League and as adviser to the secretary of the Navy designed the Navy's plan for integration. Fahy's committee oversaw the implementation of the integration of the Armed Services.

so they came up with excuses for why integration was a bad idea. "Integration will cause riots. Integration in living quarters and mess halls is not good for Negroes. We're rushing into this" were just some of the comments Symington got. "Stop the double talk and act," Symington told his generals. He advised anyone who didn't agree with the order to resign. "It's the right thing to do . . . morally . . . legally . . . militarily," he said. "And besides, the commander in chief ordered it."

General Edwards briefed the senior commanders, telling them that integration meant that blacks could be assigned to any duty for which they were qualified in any Air Force unit. Integration would begin with reassigning the most highly trained black members of the Air Force, the 332nd Fighter Wing at Lockbourne. Then black nonflying units—air cargo, military police, ammunition companies, air base security, and medical detachments—would be reassigned.

The word went down from General Edwards to senior commanders and from those commanders to lower ranking officers, "Commanders who cannot cope with the integration of Negroes into formerly white units or activities will have no place in the Air Force structure."

The Air Force integration plan called for black personnel to be screened by a review board to determine their new assignment. Screening began in May 1949. Within a few months all members of the Ohio-based 332nd had been reassigned to duty in the Far East, Europe, and the United States. By the end of the year, one third of the nearly 30,000 blacks in the Air Force had been reassigned. By May 1950, three fourths had been reassigned. The last black unit disappeared in June 1952. The Air Force integrated so rapidly and so successfully that it was nearly finished before the Army even began. It achieved this remarkable effort before American society as a whole did. In the early 1950s, the South was still segregated by law. Many other parts of the country also maintained separate schools, theaters, and other facilities for blacks and whites.

Some black Air Force personnel had misgivings as they traveled to their new assignments. They had served in seg-

Major Vernon Haywood, commander of a jet squadron during the Korean War.

regated units and were not certain if the way they did things would fit into the new integrated Air Force. Members of the 332nd compared segregation to being in a closed room in a house. Shut in their "room," they didn't really know what went on in the rest of the "house."

But they soon learned their way around the "house."

Vernon Haywood remembers a young white officer stationed at a base in Japan during the Korean War in the early fifties. Haywood, a combat veteran who had commanded the 302nd squadron in Europe, was assigned to command a squadron of 12 white pilots, fresh out of training.

"This one young man was from South Carolina. Well, I told him I was from North Carolina, right next door. He grinned. Then I told him 'we're the only Southerners here and we're surrounded by all these Yankees. We gotta really show these guys how to get things done around here.'

"I made him my assistant. He was one of my biggest boosters—an eager beaver.

"Later on, I found out that when he learned about the color of the new commander coming in, he put in for a transfer. But after the first meeting, he went over to headquarters and told them to tear up his transfer request. I didn't know anything about that at the time. We got along fabulously."

And so as it turned out, the 332nd did just fine. Colonel Davis had been a very strict commander; he made the unit "toe the mark." He had drilled his men

In everything from military courtesies, such as the proper salute, to flying combat missions. Once they arrived at their new bases and began working side by side with whites, Davis's men learned that their training had been excellent. This earned them the respect of the whites.

As they began their assignments in the integrated Air Force, the Tuskegee Airmen would credit Colonel Davis with the success of integration. He had trained them well in the 99th and the 332nd. Davis, they said, did things by the rule and he was fair.

In turn, Davis credited the combat records of the 99th and the 332nd for influencing the Air Force to give blacks a chance to prove themselves and make integration work.

In Vietnam, members of an integrated fighter group plan a mission. Left to right: Captain James Harwood, First Lieutenant James H. Manly, and Captain Robert H. Tice.

A Black Flyer in the Integrated Air Force

T   *he nation hadn't caught up with the Air Force
        when it came to integration. At his first two
stateside assignments in Kansas and California, pilot
Charles McGee had trouble finding housing for his
family. But McGee's experience with integration was
good from a military standpoint.*

1951: Major Charles McGee, is awarded the Distinguished Flying Cross by General Earl Partridge for his service as operations officer of an integrated bomber squadron in Chinhae, Korea.

"I had gone to airplane maintenance school before integration. And so my first integration assignment was officer in charge of the maintenance shop at a base in Salinas, Kansas. I had no problems with whites. Every now and then I ran into someone who was prejudiced. But they put up with the situation. There was no trouble."

Integration brought McGee into the midst of another war. He was assigned to command a fighter-bomber squadron that fought in the Korean War in the 1950s. In that war, McGee earned the Distinguished Flying Cross for several missions in which the targets were tanks, truck convoys, and guns threatening ground troops.

"During one mission, we flew

low through these valleys going after gun positions on the nearby hills. I could see my bullets hitting targets and the enemy bullets whizzing by me. Finally, one got the wing of my plane. I was losing gas but I managed to finish my strafing run and then I dropped down low and managed to make it back to the base."

After Korea, McGee was assigned to command the 44th Bomber Squadron at Clark Field in the

1966: Lieutenant Colonel McGee (second from right in front) takes winter survival training in an integrated class in Spokane, Washington.

Philippines.

"Just about all the young flying officers in the 44th were white. I remember one second lieutenant who had a medical problem that interfered with his flying status. The flight surgeon didn't want to give approval for him [the pilot] to fly because he [the surgeon] had had no experience with this kind of medical problem as it related to flying. I arranged to get the lieutenant some flying experience that proved to the flight surgeon that he [the lieutenant] could fly with no difficulty.

"That young lieutenant was Frank Borman, who later became an astronaut. So I guess we were on the right track with him. He thanked us many times both privately and publicly."

During the Vietnam War, McGee was assigned command of a reconnaissance squadron. There, while he was taking photos of enemy troop movements, his plane was damaged by enemy fire. He barely managed to land at a friendly field. He took his film out of the plane's camera and hitched a flight back to his base.

McGee went on to serve as a flight commander in Europe and in the United States, retiring as a colonel in 1973. He was one of the few pilots who flew combat missions in three wars—World War II, Korea, and Vietnam. As he looks back, McGee remembers white friends he made in Vietnam and Europe and of course his special friend Frank Borman.

"I still hear from many of them. We see each other at reunions."

1968: Major General Rollin N. Anthis awards the Legion of Merit to Lieutenant Colonel McGee for his command of a tactical reconnaissance squadron in Vietnam.

MEMORIES AND HONORS

In Arlington National Cemetery in Virginia, near the graves of other generals, is the grave of America's first black four-star general. Beneath the four stars and the flyer's wings carved into the granite is the inscription:

Daniel "Chappie" James, Jr.
General
United States Air Force
February 11, 1920–February 25, 1978

Colonel Daniel "Chappie" James, Jr., who would become the first black four-star general, is shown during a 1970 meeting with President Lyndon Johnson.

On the other side of the marker are carved the words James lived by: "This is my country and I believe in her . . . I'll protect her against all enemies, foreign and domestic."

Chappie, as everyone called him, was still a cadet pilot at Tuskegee when the 99th went into battle. When he got his wings, he was assigned to bomber pilot training with the 477th Bombardment Group stationed at Selfridge Field in Michigan. When the Air Force integrated, Chappie was sent to Clark Field in the Philippines. His Air Force career represented all that blacks hoped to achieve in the integrated Air Force. He commanded squadrons and entire combat wings during fighting in Korea and Vietnam. Rising through the officer ranks to general, he eventually was named commander of the North American Air Defense Command (NORAD), responsible for protecting the nation from air or missile attacks.

Several other Tuskegee Airmen, including Benjamin O. Davis, Jr., also would go on to earn general's stars. Many would earn colonel's eagles and command integrated squadrons in Korea and Vietnam. Some, including 332nd Fighter Group flight surgeon Vance Marchbanks and 99th Fighter Squadron pilot Marion Rodgers, joined the National Aeronautics and Space Administration (NASA). Others, like 99th Fighter Squadron pilot Lemuel Custis, left the service after the war and pursued careers in government. Custis attended law school and then served as Connecticut's chief of sales tax. Coleman A. Young, a 477th Bombardment Group gunner, was elected to the Michigan legislature, eventually becoming mayor of Detroit. Roscoe Brown, the 100th Fighter Squadron commander who flew with Davis on the historic long-distance mission to Berlin, become a college professor. Brown became the president of Bronx Community College in New York City. Willie

At a Nigerian tracking station, Vance Marchbanks (second from right), monitors the medical status of astronaut John Glenn during his February 1962 Mercury flight into earth orbit.

At the 1968 Tuskegee Airmen convention in Orlando, Florida, retired Brigadier General Noel Parrish was honored. Sitting to his left is his wife, Dr. Florence Parrish.

Ashley, a 99th pilot, became professor of biology at Howard University.

The paths of the Tuskegee Airmen have taken them in all directions since those early days. Each year, they gather in a major city for the Tuskegee Airmen Convention, a gathering of black eagles. Once they shared much, endured much, accomplished much. They gather to remember and to honor that sharing, that endurance, that accomplishment.

At a recent banquet, they shared memories:

"Remember getting that pair of wings . . . and that first salute as an officer."

"I remember I was shot down while on a strafing mission . . . I came to on the ground to find three Germans pointing guns at me."

"In this desolate boondock setting in mid-Alabama

was this functioning complete Army air base. It was like the *Wizard Of Oz and the Emerald City* or something."

"When this memo came out about integration, a group of us carrying the memo went to the Tuskegee PX dining room where only whites ate, asked for and got service."

"I'll never forget my first combat mission . . . my entry into the real war against an enemy of my country. I was frightened and proud."

They pause in their reminiscing to listen to the dinner speaker.

A young black two-star Air Force general saluted them for breaking through racial barriers. He called them the "giants onto whose shoulders I climbed to achieve." He praises them for fighting tyranny on the home front and abroad.

Charles McGee (right) was given the first Noel Parrish Gold Medallion Award at the 1989 Tuskegee Airmen Convention in Los Angeles. Here he speaks to the organization's chaplain.

A group of heroes lines up for a photo during the 1989 Tuskegee Airmen convention in Washington, D.C. Left to right: C. I. Williams, Fred Hutchins, Vernon Haywood, Luke Weathers, and Harold Sawyer. Among them they earned four Distinguished Flying Crosses and shot down four fighters during World War II.

The young general called on the Air Force heroes to inspire young people with the Tuskegee Airmen story urging them to tell the kids about the strength of Benjamin O. Davis, Jr., who endured the stony silence of his classmates during his entire four years at West Point. The speaker asked the men to remind children of Chappie's words: "I am a citizen of the United States of America and I'm no second class citizen and no man is unless he thinks like one, reasons like one, or acts like one" and to tell the young people how the Tuskegee Airmen met the challenges of their times and how they made the world a little better.

The general then read a poem he had written to honor the Tuskegee Airmen. The last two lines were: "We remember your bravery. You were the best." The general's poem is part of an exhibit at the Tuskegee Airmen Museum in Detroit.

The achievements of the Tuskegee Airmen are memorialized at several other sites. A monument at the Air Force Museum, Wright-Patterson Air Force Base,

Dayton, Ohio, tells their story. The Smithsonian Air and Space Museum in Washington features a Tuskegee Airmen exhibit. The Chappie James Science Center at Tuskegee University honors the first four-star black general. A statue in the Honor Park at the Air Force Academy in Colorado Springs carries the following inscription:

"They rose from adversity through competence, courage, commitment, and capacity to serve America on silver wings and to set a standard few will transcend."

This plaque, at Wright Patterson Air Base in Dayton, Ohio, salutes the "outstanding military service to the United States of America" of the Tuskegee Airmen.

Sources

Davis, Jr., Benjamin O. *An Autobiography: Benjamin O. Davis, Jr., American* Washington, D.C.: Smithsonian, 1991.

Francis, Charles E. *The Men Who Changed a Nation: The Tuskegee Airmen* Boston: Branden, 1993.

Gropman, Alan L. *The Air Force Integrates 1945–1964* Washington, D.C.: Office of Air Force History, 1977.

Hardesty, Von, and Pisano, Dominick. *Black Wings: The American Black in Aviation* Washington, D.C.: Smithsonian, 1983.

Hart, Philip S. *Flying Free: America's First Black Aviators* Minneapolis: Lerner, 1992.

Low, W. Augustus, and Clift, Virgil A. *Encyclopedia of Black America* New York: Da Capo, 1981.

Osur, Alan M. *Blacks in the Army Air Forces During World War II* Washington, D.C.: Office of Air Force History, 1977.

Phelps, J. Alfred. *America's First Black Four-Star General: Chappie, The Life and Times of Daniel James, Jr.,* Novato, CA: Presidio, 1991.

Sandler, Stanley. *Segregated Skies* Washington, D.C.: Smithsonian, 1992.

A bronze statue depicting a Tuskegee airman stands in the Honor Court of the Air Force Academy in Colorado Springs, Colorado.

INDEX

Photo Credits

Page 2, Charles McGee; 7, Charles McGee; 8, Smithsonian Institution; 9, Bettmann Archive; 13, Tuskegee University Archives; 14, Smithsonian Institution; 17, Charles McGee; 18, Smithsonian Institution; 22, Smithsonian Institution; 24, Archive Photos; 25, Archive Photos; 26, Archive Photos/ American Stock; 29, Charles McGee; 30, Smithsonian Institution; 32, Charles McGee; 33, Culver Pictures; 35, Charles McGee; 36, Smithsonian Institution; 37, Smithsonian Institution; 38, UPI/ Bettmann; page 39, Charles McGee; 41, Schomburg Center/New York Public Library; 45, Smithsonian Institution; 47, Charles McGee; 55, William Thompson; 61, Culver Pictures; 62, Parakeet Graphics; 65, Charles McGee; 67, Charles McGee; 68, Charles McGee; 70, Lois Marchbanks; 72, Smithsonian Institution; 73, AP/ Wide World Photos; 74, Smithsonian Institution; 75, Smithsonian Institution; 76, Charles McGee; 80, Smithsonian Institution; 82, George Watson; 87, Pima Air and Space Museum; 93, Charles McGee; 94, Smithsonian Institution; 95, Charles McGee; 96, Smithsonian Institution; 101, Smithsonian Institution; 107, Smithsonian Institution; 110, Lois Marchbanks; 113, Lois Marchbanks; 115, Charles McGee; 123, Smithsonian Institution; 125, Pima Air and Space Museum; 127, Smithsonian Institution; 128, Charles McGee; 129, Charles McGee; 130, Charles McGee; 131, Charles McGee; 132, Smithsonian Institution; 133, Lois Marchbanks; 134, Charles McGee; 135, Charles McGee; 136, Charles McGee; 137, Charles McGee; 138, Lois Marchbanks